More Praise for *The Colors* ...

"Enjoy the distilled wisdom in bite-sized ... drink deeply and you'll be wise."

— **Mark Victor Hansen**
co-creator, #1 *New York Times*
best-selling series *Chicken Soup
for the Soul*®

"Would I be asked to describe *The Colors of the Rainbow* with only one sentence, I would borrow the words of the most brilliant Indian philosopher Bhagwan Shree Rajneesh, more simply known as Osho: 'My effort is to help you to accept yourself as you are and to go searching and seeking for your authentic soul.' This book is a fountain of simple and inspiring truth that encourages women to search for their treasure within their souls, to become aware that they are already complete in themselves."

— **Sumathi Saravanan,**
software design engineer, Chennai, India

"A book for all women based on fundamental truth—beyond traditional writing."

— **Linda Sue Jones,**
office manager, Small Business Bureau,
Chicago, United States

"*The Colors of the Rainbow* reflects daily living as every woman experiences it. It shows that 'women can overcome,' that women who reach 'the mountain's peak at the end' are the managers of life. I cannot recall that men face problems as how to dress and how to look. It is easy for them: They get in a suit and that's it. Society expects women to look good while men are only expected to look average. For hundreds of years, society has expected more from women than it has from men in all areas of life. This fact might not change overnight as it is deeply rooted in the thinking of society. *The Colors of the Rainbow* is an inspiration for all women to grow spiritually and to take their lives into their hands. It encourages self-love and honesty. It is an outstanding book for women that goes beyond traditional writing. *The Colors of the Rainbow* fosters self-growth today to change society's thinking tomorrow."

— Petra Saalmueller,
Philips Corporation, and a freelance journalist , Frankfurt, Germany

"A poetic expression of a woman's journey towards light."
— Chin-Ning Chu,
international best-selling author of
Woman's Art of War

THE COLORS OF THE RAINBOW

... Eternally driven and with a longing forever new,
some of us have visited faraway places.
We have discovered beautiful treasures,
but we do not take the time to enjoy them,
nor are we ready to share.
Never has a single one of our breathless discoveries
kept our attention longer than one moment in time
and never has our search for more been completed.
Restless, we are hunting in unknown directions,
never considering where our journeys might lead
and what our motives are.
However, when we finally take courage to choose
and to discover the most brilliant colors of life
and the highest of all treasures,
we are on the most exciting journey of all time.
We will never look back,
and we will never be hunting again.
The promise is harmony and balance at the
end of the rainbow ...

THE COLORS
OF THE RAINBOW

ABOUT LIFE AND
THE BEAUTY OF LIVING

Daniela E. Schreier

One Planet Publishing House, Inc.
P.O. Box 751252
Dayton, OH 45475

www.oneplanetpublishinghouse.com
www.thecolorsoftherainbow.com

One Planet Publishing House books may be purchased for
educational, business, or sales promotion use.
For information please write:
Special Markets Department
One Planet Publishing House, Inc.
P. O. Box 751252
Dayton, OH 45475
info@oneplanetpublishinghouse.com

First Edition

Designed by Ken Clark Design Illustration Enterprise
KENCLARK77@HOTMAIL.COM

ISBN: 0-9710099-0-2

Library of Congress Control Number: 2001090360

Printed in the United States of America.

This book gives general advice and should not be relied on as a
substitute for proper medical consultation and psychological advice.
The author and publisher cannot accept responsibility for incidents or
illness arising out of the failure to seek professional therapeutic advice.

TABLE OF CONTENTS

Dedication

"Many people come into our lives and disappear without leaving any traces. A few stay with us forever." (D.S.)

This book is dedicated to my dearest friend, guide, and mentor, Chan Siew Ling. Her unique way of trusting care and loving guidance encouraged me "to plant my feet firmly on the ground" and to discover the real me, who can face life day by day.

Tommie L. Jones taught me with his very special love that dreams do come true and that, for a trusting heart, no aim is too high and no goal is unreachable.

With love and gratefulness, I remember my grandma, Erna Schmitt, who guided my first steps into this unbelievable world. She passed away much too early. It was then that I realized how precious time is and that we have limited time to spend and to share with our loved ones: It was then that I started to seize the day.

FOREWORD

As I first sat and read the manuscript of *The Colors of the Rainbow,* I was reminded of a passage in my own book *Do Less, Achieve More:* "Aimless hard work has no power to elevate you into the realm of glory that you deserve. Only by re-aligning yourself with the universal symmetry can you hope to reach your highest effectiveness. There is a rightness and a harmonious balance point within each individual and each situation." *The Colors of the Rainbow* helps us do just that. All of our striving will not get us there, we are reminded. Only in releasing ourselves and, thereby, reaching that place of ever-new joy within our hearts, can we abandon the judgments that hold us back, and keep us mortal.

This book is a fountain of simple and inspiring truths that encourage women to seek the treasures within their own souls, to become aware that they are (and have always been) complete in themselves. After reading the insightful wisdom of *The Colors of the Rainbow,* I am sure you will acknowledge this guide as an indispensable companion on your journey toward self-awareness and self-reliance.

Daniela E. Schreier, a modern professional and an exceedingly perceptive individual, blends her education in psychology with the experiences of her eventful life that have truly made her an authority on mastering existence and its fears. *The Colors of the Rainbow* is her poetic expression that serves to remind all women of their true purpose in life: to seek that Inner Balance and Harmony which only comes from getting in touch with the One Self, the Universal Source. By tapping into the ancient truths and timeless wisdom that have echoed down to us from across the myriad millennia, this book encourages women to always learn, to always think for themselves, and to experience their personal ecstatic being via the pursuit of their own, singular path.

A Himalayan sage proclaims that "relationships and life are synonymous and inseparable, that those who love the Friend within love all and are not dependent, that they are never lonely." *The Colors of the Rainbow* affirms this capacity possessed by women worldwide for deep personal growth and an ever-refined development of their interrelationships. *The Colors of the Rainbow* is a paean to serenity and self-acceptance for all women. It is a multi-hued guide that leads to the harmony and inner balance at the end of the rainbow.

— Chin-Ning Chu,
international best-selling author
of *Woman's Art of War*

TO ALL WOMEN

Time is the most precious gift. Once you give it away, it will never come back. Women dedicate more time and energy than men do to people and situations that never give back. We try to change the world, our environment, our partners. It is time to change our approaches, our attitudes, and ourselves.

All women around the world are facing similar challenges and difficulties. Our languages are different, so are our cultures and beliefs; but our struggle for love and understanding is the same.

We don't have time to learn all lessons ourselves. Let us learn and draw inspiration from the experiences of women from around the world.

It is time to let go of the old belief that the woman next door—as well as the woman thousands of miles away— is a threat, a dangerous enemy. It is time to realize that all women have the same needs and dreams. Let us share them.

The Treasure Within

Life itself is the greatest of all inspirations and the author of the world's best books. Ultimately, it is life that tells the best stories.

Whether we seek the most unbelievable of all dreams, the brightest gamma of all colors, or the saddest of all stories, we encounter them all in life. Continuous change is her only indisputable truth.

Change is the pattern of the world, and it forms the unpredictable, yet solid, structure of our lives. Change colors our lives with rich experiences.

We resist change for the longest time. Generally, we embrace powerful changes only when our pain and unhappiness have become unbearable. Only then do we become aware of the powerful tool called *choice*. We can choose our response to and our attitude about every event that occurs. In the words of William James, "Our attitude at the beginning of a difficult task will determine its successful outcome. People can alter their lives by altering their attitudes."

Life is an old and wise teacher whose lessons are stories of personal growth, compassion, and understanding. When we start to welcome and accept change in our lives, we can master new challenges and draw from our experiences. As a result, we can lovingly guide ourselves toward growth.

Change is essential in all areas of our lives, private and professional. By learning to accept things we cannot change and focusing on things we can alter by choosing a positive attitude, we become better partners and friends, more competent managers and leaders.

To accept change and to learn not to resist its consequences requires courage and the ability to let go of old behavior patterns. Often, we have to say good-bye to partners and friends because they do not grow along with us. They neither approve of nor understand the more profound self-awareness and the more positive focus in our new way of life.

Once we recognize that life is not merely about survival, but about joy and living, we might see a need to change our careers. We might start to focus on what we enjoy and do best. We will no longer try to live up to the expectations of our parents, our partners, or our social environment.

Our innermost change will be reflected in our outer lives. We will choose and attract brighter and healthier people; our social environment and relationships will improve.

Reflection and self-discovery are among the forces necessary for change. They require courage: the courage to look inside ourselves and acknowledge that we can let go of what we have now to receive what we truly need. We have to learn to live day by day in harmony with the phenomena of change and inner growth. Change works for us when we allow it to take place, to happen.

My own life changed completely in a period of 12 months. I left behind my career in the fast lane as a marketing consultant in Southeast Asia and my life as a single woman to live with my new partner in America. I started to dedicate my time to writing, returned to the university, and learned that positive change occurs naturally whenever we do not resist it.

It was necessary for me to leave behind old, self-defeating behaviors and beliefs as well as unhealthy relationships. A few true friends remained. They accepted and encouraged my positive change and growth; they welcomed a new, more self-aware, happier friend.

I am glad that life offered me a great variety of experiences, both painful and challenging. Today, I consider every one of them blessings and part of the divine pattern of learning experiences in my life. My early years in Germany and Italy, and later, my career in Southeast Asia, gave me the opportunity to live and to travel all over the world. I had to acknowledge that the mystery of life can't be solved, and I discovered that the most exciting journey—the journey of self-discovery—never ends.

The hardest lessons we learn are ultimately our greatest blessings. Our experiences always remain with us. We cannot find lasting happiness in the exterior world unless we have discovered peace and harmony inside ourselves. Neither man nor time has the power to take away our treasure, our inner beauty, for it is bound to our soul forever.

We search time and again in faraway places for fulfillment, to still our thirst and our desire for more than we have. We search the entire planet for the special treasure that could bring us contentment and relief. Yet unless we start to search inside ourselves, the treasure of our true self will be concealed from us and from the world. Each of us is a gift to the world, and each of us innately makes a difference.

If this book does inspire you to search for the treasure within, you will find that you can obtain all the colors of the rainbow. If this book can assist only one of its readers to start believing in the gift of life and in the unlimited power of her dreams, it will have fulfilled its purpose.

Trust and courage are necessary to travel the path toward realizing your dreams—and you already have both within yourself, right at this moment. Discover them and reveal them to the world. We have all made sacrifices. We have invested precious time and effort to please everyone except ourselves, often ending up ultimately disappointed.

We must each preserve our energy to search and find our hidden treasure: our soul. Then happiness will prevail. Let us accept life as the single most precious, beautiful gift and live it to the fullest.

November 30, 1999

ONCE UPON A TIME ...

"On the road toward compassion and understanding, we will learn to surrender to something greater than ourselves. The reward is extraordinary personal growth into a world that is wider than we ever could have imagined." (D.S.)

At one moment in time, we all have to face life and her facts. At that moment, we need to step back to achieve distance from our subjective life perception. We must face reality objectively. We must stop closing our eyes to our realities and start to view circumstances as they really are.

Once we stop seeing only what we want to see, facts can hit us hard. To get ourselves back on track, we need to put reality into perspective and to let go of unhealthy behavior patterns and attachments.

At times, we all try to avoid the objective state of mind. We try to escape from a realistic life view and search restlessly for more than we have, for more than we are. Often we end up confused, more insecure than before our search began.

Despite our dissatisfaction, we get stuck in a circle of excuses when it comes to taking action and causing change. We ride on the same old roller coaster of highs and lows. We get stuck with the same old problems and the same negative people time and again, unable to decide anything new or different. We try to escape, but we find ourselves back at the same starting point of an unending circle. Escape is not a solution. We need to change our attitudes and our approach to life's lessons.

Why are we so afraid of change? Why do we try to avoid it so desperately? The answer is simple: Change means discovering unknown roads, venturing into new territory. On one hand, we want to break free from existing bonds, to leave the roller coaster of repetition behind. On the other hand, we are scared to let go of old, familiar patterns. We might live a lie, stay in an unhappy relationship, or be stuck in an unrewarding career. Things might be bad, but we accept the traditional view that familiar pain is less threatening than new and unfamiliar possibilities. We are afraid of the unpredictable, so we choose predictable pain over challenging opportunities. The high price we pay for our "security" is the sacrifice of promising outcomes and the rejection of new perspectives on life.

Being courageous means overcoming old patterns. It means not blaming others for our unhappiness. We must take responsibility for ourselves and our lives, and we must learn to see the truth. It is up to us. We have choices. We can choose our attitudes and, by making choices and taking action, we can influence outcomes. It is easy to reject self-responsibility and to blame circumstances and others for our misery, but we are responsible for our own lives.

Heaven offers us choices. Experiences give us the chance to grow, to change, and to take a stand in life. The mills of heaven churn slowly and respect the human liberty to make choices. After our complaints and discontentment become unbearable, heaven makes life our teacher. Life initiates us to change and forces us to make decisions. What seems to be a defeating fiasco in the beginning often turns out to be a blessing that helps us to start over.

Life is only as good to us as we expect and accept it to be. Each of us is blessed with special gifts. While we seek far-off shores, we fail to discover the treasure within; we fail to discern special people crossing our life path.

The more we fight change, the harder it becomes. The

harder we try to make things happen—happiness, financial power, or success—the further we drive them away. The more we manipulate our partners and ourselves (Who are we kidding anyway?), the more we set ourselves up for unhappiness. It is a sad cycle that many women get stuck in and repeat for a lifetime.

What is our alternative? The alternative is called *choice* or *decision-making.* Choice is accepting the things we cannot change. Decision-making means moving on and concentrating on what we can improve. We need to let go and to allow life to unfold. It is up to us to receive pleasure and happiness from life.

Maybe things turned out differently than we wished they would have. So what? Let us agree with Frank McCourt, Pulitzer Prize–winning author of *Angela's Ashes:* "When I imagine how everything could have been, I am grateful for how everything turned out to be."

To be happy, we need to accept the fact that change is a part of life: Everything changes; nothing stays the same. It is frightening to confront change and to accept life's challenges; it is scary to learn that unfamiliar roads lead us home, to the inner self.

Change persists throughout the span of life. But the earlier we start accepting life's challenges and learning to surrender to the realities of life, the longer our happiness will last and the more we will enjoy our short trip through time.

It seems to be the self-chosen fate of many to waste a lifetime. Who would not admit in the end that being positive and accepting—instead of being negative and distressed—could have brought relief?

As we face death, our old priorities lose importance. Money and unfinished business do not matter anymore, nor does fame nor power. Death does not differentiate between the rich and the poor. It does not wait until we have completed everything on our list or been everywhere on our schedule. The sooner we realize that we must use the time we have, the longer we can celebrate the greatest inspiration of all: *life.*

THE COLORS OF THE RAINBOW

These are words, only well-meaning words.

This is all I can give to you.

You alone can give your dreams to yourself.

You alone can make your dreams come true.

Set your inner treasure free.

You alone can paint your life

in the most beautiful colors

the world has ever seen.

THE COLORS OF THE RAINBOW

The sage remembers the ancient tale of Greek mythology: In the Age of Iron, the gods had decided to create mankind. The Titan Prometheus, father of mankind, had endowed his divine spirit upon his creation.

It was not long before his sons and daughters had become the powerful masters of Mother Earth and all her creatures, obsequious only to the divine creators. Prometheus watched his children with delight and pleasure, while the 12 Olympians ruled by Zeus harbored scornful emotions for the human race.

The gods were outraged by the great achievements of their creations. The humans' accomplishments had been achieved through the divine spirit that made them the mirrors of the gods themselves.

The law of Mount of Olympus determined that the divine spirit could not be taken from Earth once it had been bestowed upon mankind. Therefore, the gods decided to hide the treasure of wisdom in a place where it would never be discovered.

A secure shelter for the divine spirit was hard to find. The gods were familiar with the intelligence and the restless drive of the earthlings. The gods of Mount Olympus believed that the humans would not stop their search for the lost treasure: No distance would be too far, no mountain too high, no sea too deep to keep their ambitious creations from trying to retrieve the lost treasure.

The mighty Zeus ruled that the hiding place of the divine spirit should be deeper than any seas and higher than any mountain ever climbed, too far from reach for mankind to discover. It had to be in a place the children of the Earth would neither know nor imagine how to reach: The spirit should be concealed within each of them. The shelter was called *soul* to mislead the earthlings. And indeed, although it was discovered by a very few humans, for thousands of years the treasure remained hidden from humanity.

Part 1

<u>RAIN OUT OF BLUE SKIES</u>

"Rain and sunshine are as necessary
and essential for our personal growth
as they are for the rainbow to show
its most beautiful colors." (D.S.)

There can't be sun and light without rain and darkness: All are part of the cycle of nature. The rainbow appears only after the rain, sometimes heavy rain.

To reach the mountain peak, we must begin our climb in the valley. To reach the fundamental truth that life is the greatest gift of all, that our happiness lies within us, we have to understand and to know ourselves first, to master the most difficult personal situations. The obstacles along the way often seem overwhelming. But they are never too difficult to master as long as we accept them as necessary and useful parts of our life experience: events that we can draw strength from, that will form our character and embolden us.

We begin by walking through the valley, but soon we are able to climb, passage by passage, to the peak. On our way through the valley, we gain indispensable experiences in all fields of life. We are initiated into our basic life roles during our childhood. We are daughters, friends, and sportswomen first. Later we learn to play the responsible parts of lovers, parents, and business partners. Our roles become broader. Our responsibilities toward society and ourselves grow on our journey through life; and the motivating power of love plays its role throughout the various stages of our life.

The role of the eternal student remains with us always. We are confronted with life's ever-changing lessons. While the settings and actors change, the basic lessons will be repeated. Life is a patient teacher: Unless we master our lessons by recognizing and correcting our patterns, we must learn the same lessons again and again.

Life does us the favor of repeating what we have not understood in the first place; she helps us with extra instruction until we learn to choose the right response. Once we understand that it is up to us, we can learn to trust ourselves, to choose our replies and our reactions.

Basically, there is no good or bad experience except as it is determined in our mind. Let us separate joyful delight from painful sorrow. Could we distinguish joy and happiness from sadness without knowing the meaning of both emotions? How could we respect and expect loving care and warmth without having discovered painful neglect?

To appreciate and discover life at its fullest, we have to be aware that both delight and sorrow are unavoidable parts of life. Looking back, we must admit it was often painful experiences that helped us to grow while positive experiences encouraged us to continue on our way. Both helped us to discriminate, to set boundaries, to build, and to trust our internal voice. Step by step, we are led to self-acceptance and respect: respect first for ourselves and then for others.

➤ Taking Leave and Finding the Strength to Go On

I will always remember that phone call, the message that reached me on a cold October evening. I had arrived in England from one of the hottest summers known on Italy's Adriatic coast. It was mid-September. I had stopped in Germany to see my grandparents, who had raised me. I exchanged suitcases and went straight from Frankfurt to Birmingham. The flight was a disaster, and it was the first ever journey by airplane for me. I reached the huge Frankfurt airport after an hour's delay and barely made it through the departure hall.

The flight had been delayed because of an overcast sky

and heavy rain. I found myself airborne, tired and overwhelmed, but thanking God (of whom I had a very unclear picture in those days). I had made it even after airlines counter agents and check-in personnel had told me, "Sorry, too late." I had made it against all odds.

Aristocratic England welcomed me with a chilling cold. It would last for the next three months as I learned to treasure my long, gray winter coat. Also chilling was the English's outspoken belief in the traditional superiority of the Anglican nation and in her independence from the European Community. Proudly, they still believed in the Commonwealth.

Only much later did I learn to put such beliefs and individuals' opinions in perspective and view them for what they were: opinions and ideas expressed by separate people, not to be generalized and not to be acclaimed if not shared by all.

It is understandable—because I was a young woman with idealistic notions who loved warm weather—that the English climate was initially irritating to me. Indeed, I questioned my choice to live there many times. However, it is part of human nature to adapt to surroundings and environmental realities.

Change and new experiences eventually broaden our horizons by exposing us to the new and different. The challenge has to be accepted. The secret lies in trying to understand others, to relate to them and to new circumstances, to feel more compassionate and more courageous, to live new experiences and to share your life.

Initially, I had a hard time getting over the weather and the English lifestyle, especially people with prideful opinions of their country. Sometimes I was not sure if anyone had realized that Great Britain's imperialism was over.

However, this did not diminish the important learning experience I gained from my temporary duties as an assistant language teacher. The monthly paycheck was reasonable, and I had no cause to leave my three-month assignment at Park Hall School.

Once I had decided to live these three months as a new experience and to accept the period of time as an opportunity to widen my own world picture, I stopped suffering through each day. I was ready for my first venture into the storybook of my own life.

All of these memories are associated with that October phone call, which changed my life forever. I picture myself in the dark, narrow hall of the two-story, semi-detached English house, where I had rented a tiny room. When I picked up the phone, I began a "taking leave" that took 15 months and that brought the greatest ever grief and loss to my life.

I was about to lose the one person who had taught me everything, who had taught me life itself, who had initiated me on the first steps of my journey. This strong and most modern woman had always insisted on the importance of my studies and my future goals.

I was about to lose my beloved Grandma, who had shared my life forever, who had raised me.

Before my departure to England, it had seemed that finally, after the long years of my grandfather's illness, after severe financial struggles and the loss of enterprise and estate, life would bestow freedom for my grandparents. However, at that very moment, the time gifted to my grandma was about to run out, to come to an unexpected end.

The minute I took the call, I felt that something was frighteningly different. My grandfather was on the line. He and I used to talk, but it was always my grandma who did the calling. She would talk to me first, and my entire life it had been that way, no matter where I was.

My grandfather's voice was filled with concern and anxiety as he explained to me that my grandma had seen a specialist for lung diseases. She had never been sick in her adult life and had never taken the time to rest, to relax, and to think about herself and her own well-being.

Today, I ask myself what is more urgent and important than our well-being? What else has more urgency? I can't remember my grandmother ever complaining. She was rescued as a baby from a deadly infection, and ever since then, she had perceived her life as a gift.

She had visited a specialist for a routine examination six months earlier. A small black spot was found on her lungs, which was diagnosed as benign, and she was told that a routine exam twice a year would do. My grandma had never smoked a cigarette in her entire life. However, during the previous weeks, she had suffered from breathing problems. She had never mentioned one word of this to me over the phone. Water in the lungs was diagnosed. It had to be removed immediately, and we could only hope it would not return.

When my grandmother came to the phone, I could hear her firm voice shaking and literally see the tears in her eyes. The rest is history.

When I returned home for Christmas, the water had already been removed twice and kept returning to her lungs. She was seen by a clinic specializing in lung diseases, where she had been operated on earlier. The doctors said that it was now too late, that they could do nothing more for her. The cancer had spread throughout her body, and they gave her three months to a year to live. She was released from the hospital and told that everything would be fine, but I was left to know the horrible truth.

I will never forget her smile when she was informed that she could return home, despite her pain and the need for ongoing therapy. The doctor told her she could eat whatever she desired. My grandmother was a very positive person who loved life and, aside from her professional assets, she was a brilliant cook who delighted in preparing and sharing meals with others.

She looked happy, and during that time, I enjoyed remembering various stories of her youth. She was a teenager during the years of the Third Reich in Hitler's Germany. When she was 15, her father accompanied her on a journey far away from their home so she could attend an academy for teachers. However, the Sudetenland, an area of Silesia, was soon under attack because Hitler was fighting to expand Germany beyond her borders. Her dream of becoming a teacher ended with the beginning of the war. She had to flee from the institute, leaving her studies and the university behind, and the war abruptly ended the dreams of that bright young girl. But she did not ever give up. Following the war, the misery was horrendous, and she could not return to school. She managed to find an apprenticeship in Bad Kissingen, close to her village in Bavaria, where she became a secretary, an accountant, and then an office manager.

Her resilience taught me to make the best of each situation in my life. She was able to accept reality, to make decisions, and to live with them.

Other stories about her sprang to life in my memories: She obtained her driver's license in the early 1950s, a revolutionary act for a woman in the years immediately after the war, when it was still the unwritten prerogative of men to drive. Soon after her marriage to my grandfather, she left her job as an accountant. The two of them jointly founded a small construction company, and my grandma managed the office.

For years, I wondered about the opposing traits and behavior patterns of the two individuals who had decided to form a partnership for a lifetime and who had raised me from childhood.

My grandmother was positive and strong while my grandfather was pessimistic and a procrastinator. He had difficulty letting things go and getting on with life, and he never found closure with his hurtful childhood.

Especially in the later years, my grandmother seemed to carry lots of responsibility. She was a woman who could endure deprivation and pain. She would always stand straight while Grandpa was a jaded critic.

When I looked at her near the end of her life, as she was just returning from the hospital, I could see that her spirit was unbroken and full of hope. I returned her smile, bidding my eyes to hold back the tears. Tragic things happen to people—even to people we love—every day. The unique part of this situation was not only that it was happening to the person I loved most, but also that I could not or would not share my grief and knowledge of her terminal diagnosis of cancer with anybody as the disease approached its final stage.

No one except me knew the shattering truth. I had spoken to the senior consulting physician who had been taking care of my grandmother, and news of the diagnosis never left the room.

I had to do what seemed best to me. My grandfather had been sick for years with liver cancer, and his sole reason for living was my grandmother. He had been forced to give up his own business, and he was too worn out to work at any other job. Frustrated by the state of affairs in the country and angry at the government, he had given up on life. It was my grandmother who optimistically showed him the pleasure they still could find and share in day-to-day living, especially in the small pleasures of life.

In the beginning, I tried to kid myself: Maybe everything was going to be fine; the analysis might have been wrong. I wanted to live day by day. I believed I could make time stop or make it pass so slowly that a year could become 10, 15, 20—or forever. Every night in my bed, I cried, but I was smiling during the day.

The questions "Why her?" and "Why in such a tragic way?" seemed unavoidable. They crossed my mind millions of times in those months. I was still attending the university, and I had the chance to participate in an Erasmus Exchange Program in Italy for one semester. It seems a paradox, but I accepted it. I was always strongly involved in my studies and later in my jobs, which helped me to forget, to escape until the late night came. As grief haunted me over the years, it would ultimately catch up with me late at night, not allowing me to rest.

My strong will to build a better future and to find a meaning in life helped me through this difficult period. I had to escape from time to time; otherwise, it seems as if the grief would have killed me.

Losing the one person who meant everything to me was the greatest challenge I had ever overcome in my life. I tried to apply the principles of my grandmother, who taught me not to give up no matter what might come. She taught me that bonds reach beyond the visible and existing world.

The time I spent in Italy away from her actually brought me closer to her. It helped me to focus on my life. To hear her voice over the phone brought me joy. Also, I knew I could not accompany her on her last journey. I could only appreciate and be thankful for the time remaining to us. Every day became precious. Whether near or far from one another, whether talking over the phone or going for a walk together, we were in touch.

By the time her funeral came, I had run out of tears, for I had taken leave of her long before. People thought that I was being as cold as ice, but that did not matter to me. Some battles we must fight alone.

The time of taking leave was a very important period in my life. I learned to accept that we can't keep the people and things we love forever. We are not in charge of time. Change—even change as painful as experiencing a loved one's death—is necessary for us to grow. Change is un-avoidable. Nothing stays the same for eternity. Evolution requires change. Drastic, painful changes are the most valuable experiences in our lives because they challenge us to grow spiritually.

I prayed hard, asking for a reason, some justification for losing my grandma. I felt despair and anger. I buried my-self in endless work. But we can never run away and close our eyes to change: It will ultimately catch up with us.

Today, I know it would have been easier if I had shared knowing that her disease was terminal. I could have shared that reality with my grandmother from the beginning. It would have made it easier for both of us. She might have known anyway, deep in her heart, that there would be no return to health and that the trial of death would soon visit her. I was too scared to talk about it. For a long time, I felt helpless and guilty. I thought I had left her alone with her insecurity about an unknown future.

I tried to show her that I would be able to manage alone. I felt guilty because I could never give back to that great woman what she had offered to me: her life.

Only after a decade had passed could I let it rest and accept the unchangeable past, accept that everything was perfectly all right then. I do not feel guilty anymore, as I did for years, because I have learned to accept the fact that, during the time of her disease, I could not have done better. I could not have performed better or endured more than I did.

Today, because I have more experience and understanding, I could behave differently. I could be of more help to my grandmother and myself because I have grown and I have learned many wonderful lessons about pain, anger, and frustration. Back then, my feelings were frozen, and I was numb. After her death, I would allow no one to get close to me. I wanted to protect myself from pain. I did not know that by preventing myself from loving and being loved, I was depriving myself of a new chance for happiness.

Before her death, I had tried to avoid reality by avoiding the truth: the unchangeable truth about her inevitable death. Not talking about it and not sharing it made the truth my own secret, trapping me for the time being in my pain and my loss. Over the following years, I learned to share happiness and pain, joy and sorrow, fear and disappointment.

Looking back, I realize that I could not have shared any of my feelings with my grandfather. Because of his serious alcohol problem, his ailing body, and his self-pity, he could not be supportive of my grandma. Only much later could I deal with the fact that he was a very sick man. My grandfather was a restless person. A lifetime of continuous worrying had deprived him of happiness. Because of his heavy drinking, he rejected the good things in life and saw only the negative side of events. He ignored the advice of his doctors and, as a result, he brought several crises and emergencies upon himself.

My grandmother helped him back on his feet time and again. For short periods, he resisted his negative inclinations and seemed to have learned his lesson. But never for long. Soon, he would start his downward spiral all over again. I view his behavior objectively today. I understand that he was hurting, unable to escape the eternal roller coaster of highs and lows in his life, unable to find peace or rest. He was unable to face life and unable to love and treasure himself. It took time to forgive him for his untamed moods. Those same moods in me controlled my life until I realized that I, not my moods, have power over my life, that I, not my negative thoughts, am the decision maker in my life.

This book has been strongly inspired by my childhood experiences. It was painful at times to be caught between the strong character of my grandma and the volatile moods of my grandpa, but my childhood was a rewarding, useful, and very unique human experience. Today I am grateful for those two people, for their guidance and their strength that led me to find my own life.

Today, I know that my grandfather loved me, that he played the cards he was dealt the best he could. It took time for me to resolve my hurt over the verbal abuse and dark moods, but finally I learned to recognize his behavior for what it was: unhealthy and self-defeating. I fought my way through it and grew. I grew spiritually and emotionally, knowing that I could control my own moods, that I could be positive and happy.

The path and the approach to life that I have chosen are very different from those my grandparents chose. The fact remains that a loving heart never loses its treasures; it only misplaces and then rediscovers them. Most importantly, the tragic, slow death of my grandmother made me more human, more compassionate, more appreciative of others and their fears—and of myself.

At the very end, Grandma was admitted to the hospital yet again. A new doctor proposed one more operation and chemotherapy. My grandmother's response had always been a yes to life. She must have known that her sickness was terminal, and this time, her knowledge was confirmed by the doctor's frankness with her about the seriousness of her illness. She went through her last painful trial and died shortly after her first sessions of chemotherapy at the hospital.

I was there the final night with her, holding her hand, saying good-bye again, this time forever. I was worried because the priest was not with her as she died. Today I know that it did not matter.

I now have a stronger foundation, a belief that is at the same time broader and more individual than the Roman Catholic views I was brought up with. I believe in a Higher Power that is always with me. I call him my Father. He knows and sees everything and is the creator of the beautiful universe. He is not allied with any particular religion, and we pray to him in different languages and worship him with different rituals. Loving, sharing, and caring are what make us human and bring us closer to God, regardless of our culture or race. We have emphasized for too long what separates us. It is time to realize the simple fact that being human unites us. I believe God wants us to be united and at peace with one another. I believe he is always with us, giving us powerful experiences and speaking to us through our inner voices.

I know that my grandma did not need the priest, as she

could simply not wait any longer. God was there with us. She was a beautiful person, and I found a sense of something holy in her suffering. We had been given a life filled with beautiful experiences together. We were given more than a year to say good-bye.

She never lost her faith even in the last months of life. She was always happy and proclaimed that life was a special gift to her. In fact, everybody had given up on her when she was two years old. At that time, a high fever threatened to take her away, but a courageous doctor inspired by a divine power saved her life by opening the air passageway at her throat that had caused the fever. She survived and was given a second chance at life. She saw me grow up and go my own way, and we said good-bye 60 years after her first brush with death.

She was a good person who had fewer human flaws than any other person I know. Sometimes she was tough, as tough as life required, but she was always happy and trusting in her heart. What more can there be?

Our loved ones will always leave us too early; time spent together will never be enough. My grandma died when I was 20, but we had more time than we could ever have expected. I was blessed. The mystery of life had offered me the opportunity to grow up with this wonderful woman. Grandma's philosophy: "In the end, we are only around for a quick cup of coffee. Enjoy it!"

I thank her dearly for having taught me that giving and sharing bring more happiness than receiving. I thank her for helping me to be more open, to show my feelings, to hold someone's hand, or to take someone in my arms. Today I empathize with a good friend in trouble or a person who thinks she's lost everything because of the end of a love affair or some other tragedy. After many years, I have learned to listen more and to talk less.

As I have come to accept my own grief and my own feelings, I have learned to be more compassionate and not so harsh with other people. These lessons were time-consuming, but I have become a better person by over-coming the low self-esteem that I had experienced with my grandfather's behavior.

My grandfather died only six months after Grandma. I saw him for the last time in the days after my grandma's funeral. He was devastated. We were both alone in our grief, existing separately in our own worlds. Externally, I seemed very strong. I did not show my pain or hurt. I was aggressive and insensitive toward my grandfather, who aged dramatically in his final months.

I remember once sitting at his bed telling him, "Don't you know it is hard for me also? I lost my grandma, the one person who meant so much to me. I know exactly how you feel."

Finally, I departed for Italy, where my new job was waiting. In order to make a living, I had given up attending the university after two years. Only in the eight years that followed did I recognize that merely making a living and surviving are not enough.

Before I left for Italy, I asked Grandpa to join me and live with me abroad. The weather would always be nice, I told him. I knew that he loved sunshine and a temperate climate. His sad reply: "The roots of an old tree can't be transplanted into foreign soil."

During the next six months, he was in and out of hospi-tals—and finally he died. Actually, he had decided to end his life. He fell victim to the influence of false friends, al-cohol, hopelessness, and despair. His search for meaning was over. Life had become a burden to him. Could my presence have made a difference? I don't know, and I have stopped asking myself that question.

I remember the day I called the hospital and the doctor told me that Grandpa had died in the early morning hours. I replied that he had died exactly six months before: when he had lost the meaning of his existence, gave up on his willingness to live, abandoned thoughts of the future, and was left without any goal in life. The day he lost his life was the day he lost my grandmother.

I was angry at my mother, whom I believed did not care about any of this during all that time. Today the anger is gone, and I am no longer judgmental.

After Grandpa's funeral, I never returned to our home. I never entered our apartment again. Long before, my grandparents had sold all our property to pay off old debts, and we had lived in a simple apartment. My horror and my inner pain were too huge and were holding me back from making a visit.

I am holding in my memories both my grandmother, as a brilliant, hearty teacher of life, and my grandfather, as the best parent he could be considering his sad, abusive youth and his negative worldview. I gave up all rights to the apartment; I did not return to the grave that holds only their bodies.

Today I know that everything fits perfectly in the divine pattern of life. The early loss of my loved ones taught me to deal with change and pain. Scared and frightened in the beginning, I focused on my job, and I managed to take care of myself. I adopted the principle I learned from my grandma and made the best of each situation. Over time I also learned that a job must bring both fulfillment and financial reward. I returned much later to my university studies. It took me a very long time to open up my heart again. I feared ever feeling pain and sorrow again.

Only recently have I become open to love and romance. I learned to let go of the fear and to embrace abundance, and I dared to make the important decision to share my life. It took me 10 years to be able to do that.

I know that my grandma is happy for me today. I know because our bond is not broken, and I still talk to her after all this time.

Viktor E. Frankl remarks in his bestseller, *Man's Search for Meaning,* that it is the difficult, external situations that give man the opportunity to grow spiritually beyond himself. He states that we need to take life's tests seriously, that we must not give up because if we do give up on life, we die. My grandfather died because he had lost his meaning for life—my grandma.

Despite my overwhelming grief, I felt life had given me a chance to grow, and I knew that the spirit of my grandma was still around as was my Higher Power. In those days, when everything that mattered to me had been taken away, I knew that nothing worse could happen. I concentrated on building a life—my life. Ever since the death of my grandmother, I have held onto the firm impression that a special protecting angel is watching me from above, and I always feel safe along the way.

Grandmother would probably smile today at my wish to pass on my experiences for others with open hearts and minds to evaluate, at my wish to share with those who might choose to draw from my observations. Grandma always argued that people attending the school of life need more than academic knowledge: They need education of the heart.

Even more than children or the poor might need it, we adults living in the fast lane of modern society require education of the heart. By listening to our hearts, we can over-come our spiritual losses, our internal pain, and our yearn-ing for true meaning that seems to elude us in an environ-ment of material wealth.

Years after the death of my grandparents, life taught me that loss is not always a result of death. We can lose friends by ending a relationship, and the loss might be temporary or forever. When I lost a splendid friend in Singapore, I was full of resentment; I blamed the circumstances. That loneliness was very different from what I experienced after my grandparents' deaths.

Actually, how do we measure pain, grief, loneliness, and other intense emotions? We cannot measure our pain and hurt, but we can access whatever amount of energy we need to pick ourselves up again and to get back on track on the road called life.

➢ **Setting Boundaries**

Accepting values and setting and allowing boundaries are the foundations for lifelong friendship, trust, and inti-macy. If we do not respect each other's boundaries—which means respecting our values and our emotional and physi-cal limits—we put our friendships and relationships at risk. What remains if we lose a relationship in this way is a bitter memory of a once special bond. Such losses should not be allowed to happen.

My friend Mara, one of the most pleasant people I have ever met, went through a difficult time. Her background included a forced marriage to a man she had never loved. She, however, had not given up on life. She focused her life on her gratifying job in one of Singapore's important shopping centers, her two beautiful children aged five and eight, and some good friends with whom she could share her sorrows.

After years of silent acceptance, she had finally found the courage to break the legal bonds of her strict Muslim marriage. She was ready to start life all over, to confront the word *divorce.*

For most Europeans or Americans, marriage is associated with love and with the free choice of both partners. Divorce creates a storm of hurt feelings. The disappointment and pain of a failed relationship are accompanied by doubt and self-blame. Divorce, which is often accompanied by a painful, nerve-wracking legal procedure, causes enormous emotional stress. It is certainly more difficult for a woman than for a man to obtain a divorce under Sharia Law, the Islamic legal and religious law on marriage and divorce—especially when the family has children and particularly when the husband does not want a separation. The husband has to agree to a divorce in the first place; otherwise, it is not possible to obtain one. He has to divorce his wife before the Muslim court by saying three times, "I divorce you." Then the act is legally sanctioned. This is not a critique of the Islamic legal system and procedures, but only an explanation of what was waiting for Mara.

Before the actual divorce, Mara had gone through years of unfulfilled marriage, a long period of counseling at the Muslim court, and endless discussions with her own family. The fact is, her father had arranged for and forced her into a marriage she did not want. Finally, he was on her side, agreeable to the separation.

The first step to be taken was that Mara had to move out of the apartment she shared with her husband—and she had to leave her children behind. The children, of course, were her main concern. There was a probability under Muslim law that custody would go to the father, that Mara's leaving the family premises, as a first step of separation, would influence the judge's opinion about her maternal abilities.

Mara was financially and emotionally the primary supporter of her family. She left her apartment, and her Indonesian housekeeper stayed behind to take care of the children.

Having a housekeeper is not a luxury in Asia. It is very affordable, as the monthly wage for a foreign domestic worker does not exceed $300, and, at least in Singapore, half goes to the government and half to the foreign worker. The Philippine or Indonesian maids live with the family, sharing the children's room or staying in a small area attached to the kitchen.

After she left her apartment, Mara had no place to stay and little money to spend. A couple of her friends offered her a refuge, but she felt uncomfortable; she did not want to intrude. I was living alone and had a spare bedroom available. I suggested that Mara stay with me, offering a temporary solution. I did not insist upon setting a time limit or a rental agreement. I thought friends should not have to establish clear guidelines. I trusted that things would work out.

As time passed, we got used to each other's company during the evenings. It was challenging at times, for Mara was used to living in a large Asian family while I had lived alone for over 10 years. I was short-tempered at times and was often irritated in the mornings. Usually I was struggling to make it on time to the taxi waiting downstairs, which would bring me to my first meeting, while upstairs, I was going between my in-house office, the shower, and a cup of coffee.

Basically, however, everything went fine, and we were somewhat happy together. In the meantime, we had made an agreement concerning Mara's children visiting and staying overnight. Because I worked from my home, I needed to be informed before the children would visit and stay the night. It was turbulent, but also exciting, to have a family all of a sudden.

One night Mara came back with the three children without having made prior arrangements with me. I heard them coming into the house, and I confronted Mara and called her to my room. I felt bad that I had to remind her of our agreement, that I had to tell her once again that my office was at the apartment, that I had to earn a living. Mara gave me many valid reasons for her having her children over, all reasons I understood. I reminded Mara that a phone call before coming over would have kept our promise and would have been respectful of my privacy. That one time, I accepted her having the children over even though our agreement had been broken.

As Mara's stay approached its fifth month, I was no longer sure if she had any intention of looking for her own place. I became very upset but kept my anger inside. Her separation and her counseling period were still ongoing, and I felt sympathy for my friend's situation.

I was facing financial problems. I had been having cash flow problems as I started my own business, and I had gone through a fearful period of financial instability. Even though I secured orders for my suppliers from overseas, I would have to wait for months to obtain my commission payments. I felt stressed by bills and credit cards needing to be paid. I did not know how to handle my own situation and avoided asking my friend about her plans. I started to consider renting out Mara's room for about $400 per month, money that would have been a financial help to me.

Today I know it would have been best to discuss the situation. We could have determined that Mara had to move out in a timely manner or that she should have begun to contribute to the rental payment. It would have saved our friendship.

Finally it happened. I needed money badly for a business trip overseas in order to accompany some clients to see some marble quarries in Sicily. My credit cards were at their limit; I could not afford to lose the business. I confided in Mara. She gratefully helped me with $1,500, money from her little daughter's savings, and I told her I would pay her back as soon as possible.

Then, during the seventh month of our shared living arrangement, her boyfriend visited from Ireland. Mara had met this man, who obviously adored her, several months before. I agreed that during his short visit, they could stay at the apartment. We had still not put a time limit on Mara's stay in my house, and I had not brought up that she needed to pay rent. I thought a friend should not ask for payment. Wrong! But back then, I thought it would have cast a shadow over our friendship. I did not know that clarity would have served our relationship better than resentment.

Vincent arrived. Mara had already told me about their bad experience during his previous visit a month before. While staying at the house of another female friend, they faced problems with "privacy." Mara told me, in fact, that her friend had exposed herself to Vincent. Hotels are not cheap in Singapore, so I agreed that they could stay in my home.

He arrived in the middle of September as I was due to

leave for work in Italy. Mara fetched Vincent from the airport, and I quickly prepared some pasta to welcome my guest. After a pleasant evening, I left the next night for Rome, leaving them behind alone. I was very busy and had increasing financial problems, but I had agreed with Mara that she would have to pay at least her share of the phone bill and the electricity.

However, I did not confront her with my ever increasing feelings of discomfort over her staying at my place without a time limit and without her making a rental contribution. I had expected her eventually to tell me how long she would stay and how she thought about resolving her housing problems. I felt that she could stay with me and pay a fixed monthly rent, or that she should give me an indication of when she wanted to move out. I thought that, because we were friends, we would automatically think alike, that we had consideration and respect for one another, and the same boundaries.

This is not ever true. We are unique human beings, and no two of us think and feel alike. Today, I would simply talk openly about the situation with her. Back then, I could not, and it was fatal to our friendship.

I was still in Italy when Mara informed me that Vincent had finished his visit. I was happy that she had found someone who cared for her, and I was aware that she was going through a challenging period in her life. We were in touch over the phone all the time, but I still did not have the courage to talk to her about the boundaries we needed to draw in order to save our friendship. Not bold enough to speak up, I expected her to be the one to clear the air.

It is a common misassumption for a woman to think she knows exactly what her counterpart is thinking and what her friend's words mean. But do we often really hear what the other party has to say, or do we just hear what we want to hear, presuming whatever we want to presume? It would be so much easier to step up to the other person and share our true concerns. Many friendships and relationships could be rescued with a straightforward discussion. Instead, we sometimes complain to third parties who are not involved in the situation, stating how helpless we are and how ruthless our friend is. When I poured my heart out to another friend in this instance, I was advised wisely: "Go and talk to Mara; straighten things out. You are responsible for yourself first, then for others."

Two days before I returned home, Mara informed me that her boyfriend had returned unexpectedly from Ireland. I was stunned. She had finally obtained her divorce, and they had plans to get engaged. Vincent again stayed at my place, but this time my approval was not asked for.

I wonder if the situation was my fault because I made everything seem so natural and agreeable. I wonder if I had been too mellow. I had expected my boundaries to be respected without drawing them first. "Vincent was a man old enough that he should know how to act," I thought, transferring my anger from Mara to him. I did not consider that I had allowed them the opportunity to violate my boundaries in the first place—because I hadn't made my boundaries clear. I recognize today that if we do not set our limits clearly enough, we risk being disrespected.

Finally I called Mara to tell her that we would need to discuss our living situation once I came back. At that time, I did not sense any concern on her part. Maybe I was mistaken or maybe she just didn't see that my tolerance had reached an end.

I arrived in Singapore, moody and extremely tired. When I arrived home, I found several pairs of men's boots in front of my house and a notebook computer and documents that were not mine in my living room.

"His things are all over," I thought. It was more than I could bear. That evening I had a dinner appointment, and I was actually happy to leave my apartment, where I felt like a tolerated guest.

The attitude toward my visitors changed. I was no longer warm and welcoming, and I knew it would have an effect. I agreed with Mara to have a heart-to-heart talk the next afternoon, and she was more than an hour late. Finally, I knocked at the door to remind her of our appointment. She answered tensely, saying that she would come out in a couple of minutes.

When I explained to her that I had shared my frustrated feelings with a friend, who advised me to talk to her, Mara was offended that I had discussed the situation with another person in the first place. And she had a point: I should have talked to her from the start. I should have set my boundaries before she moved into my house.

I requested a time frame determining her length of stay, and I told her that my financial situation was not good enough to pay for the apartment alone. She answered that I should have told her more about my business situation and that she did not know about my financial dilemma. I explained that receiving orders from clients did not mean that I would obtain immediate cash payment. Anyway, I said, the problem was not my commissions or my cash flow. Even if my financial situation had been sound, I asked, wasn't she aware that our friendship was at stake?

She informed me that Vincent felt that the room did not offer sufficient space for them, and therefore they would look for an apartment. "Good," was all I could say, "do it fast."

Vincent did not leave the room that evening or the next morning; and the door to their room remained closed. The invisible man in my spare bedroom imprisoned himself in my house.

The situation was escalating, and we had not yet settled our accounts: Mara had to pay the rest of her share of the phone and electric bills while I owed her the $1,500 she had loaned me earlier.

After my discussion with Mara, I sat in my living room for a long time trying to figure out why things had happened the way they did. They happened that way because we procrastinated in the first place, because we let them escalate without dealing with the reality we faced. Shouldn't we have addressed the problems before they became major issues? A simple discussion on the rules of moving in and sharing an apartment would have sufficed to avoid what became a crisis. Revision of the agreement after three months of her living there for free would have been sufficient to respect each other's needs. This lesson taught me that true friends understand clear words and accept boundaries.

I left a note at Mara's door, telling her I would need to charge her $500 for the seven months she had stayed in my home. It broke my heart to do that, but my financial situation required some minimal payment from her. Mara left payment for her share of the phone bill on the table, but also a note saying she would not be happy about the amount I wanted to withhold for rent because it was money she had put aside for her daughter. She claimed I should have told her in the first place that rental payment would be necessary.

The next day, I left a check for $1,000 on the table. I let Mara know that she would be able to cash the check after eight weeks because, by then, my commissions would be deposited into my account.

Mara and Vincent planned on moving out the following Sunday. In the meantime, their door remained closed; I again felt like an intruder within my own four walls. Finally, they changed their moving plans to Saturday. Mara's belongings stored in my storeroom and the items in her room all had to be moved.

We talked briefly. Mara was sorry; I was sorry. I went to Mara's room. Her boyfriend was inside. I told him: "This is nothing personal, and I wish you both good luck." He replied sharply: "I do not want to be involved in that. But it is your fault too." I lost my temper and advised Mara to get him out of my house immediately. Mara was close to tears when I left the room.

My phone rang, and it was my best friend, Siew Ling. While I was on the phone, the door to my house closed. Mara had left. I am not sure if she knocked at my door to say good-bye. She had left for good.

I called her cellular phone only minutes after her departure and left a message on her answering machine: "I do care for you and your children and I wish you happiness and luck. Go slow with Vincent. You are just out of a relationship. Call me back!"

I never heard from Mara, but I still think of her. I tried to call her cell phone before I left Singapore, but the number was out of service.

After more than 18 months, I sent a letter to her workplace and someday I will call her office. Friends always remain in our hearts, even after difficulties.

Can people start over by establishing new rules and clear boundaries? Can we mend by speaking openly and not running away from our problems? Can any of us save the world with more compassion and love? I believe we can make a difference. At the very least, we can make the world, at least our small part of it, a better place to live in and to be who we truly are.

We need to choose our friends wisely, but before blaming them we have to look inside ourselves. What we despise most in them might actually be quite familiar to us as a part of our own character. We need to harness our own power first, to love ourselves, and to respect ourselves. Then we can listen and understand instead of judging. Friendship is more than just a word: It is a huge responsibility. It is a two-way street that requires giving and taking. I believe that only very few people in our lives can share that special bond with us, where words are rarely needed, where an unspoken thought or a look says it all. With the other 99 percent of the world, our acquaintances and "social friends," it is necessary to talk, to send clear signals, and to set firm boundaries.

The human brain is far more powerful than any computer. The "program" that another person's brain is "running" is very individual and different from ours. It is impossible for us to obtain detailed data without learning about the other person and listening to him or her. Often we have presumed beforehand in our minds what our friends think or mean. Instead, from the very beginning of every situation, we must stop, *listen,* and try to understand before we make decisions and take actions.

➤ Divine Order

I had just gotten the news that the supply contract I was working on for the previous three months had been awarded to another company. My client told me that it was nothing personal, that my competition simply could fulfill the contract at a lower price. Now what?

The human mind eagerly plans each step along the way, working hard to predict an outcome—even though it cannot be known—and clinging desperately to its desires. Still, things happen differently than we plan for them to. They develop in a direction we could not have fathomed. Life seems to be hard on us at times. We need to accept that divine patterns are unpredictable. We need to trust in the inevitability of a positive outcome. We need to be aware that what seems to be a setback might be ultimately to our advantage, a blessing and a valuable experience.

How often do we work hard and invest all of our thoughts and energy on things we believe to be necessary to our future, including relationships, friendships, and careers? We work and plan only to find—after all of our best efforts—that our wishes do not always come true. They do not work out the way we wanted them to. How much energy do we devote to planning out fantasies? We know what to say when these fantasies become reality, but often they do not. Sometimes they are only delayed, but sometimes they never come to pass.

We ask ourselves why, why me? Often we feel despair and anger. We feel powerless and betrayed. Let us remember the despair and the resentment we felt when we were not admitted to our favorite university, when we were not chosen for a promotion, when our long-term partner left us, or when we felt betrayed.

It is difficult to see in these emotional difficulties the opportunity to grow and widen our horizons. Some of us blame ourselves; others search for an explanation that might remain unattainable.

With time and some distance and trust, we learn to understand that the divine pattern works in our lives. The answers will come. Weeks, months, and even years later, we come to understand that the entire plan of life has worked out. We lose our attachment to one single view of life. We might be in a much better position long after the situation that disturbed us is over. We might have kind friends and find ourselves in a rewarding relationship. We might not have any of this had our own original plan come true.

Time shows us the truth. Patience and trust in a positive outcome help us to let go and let God in. In the meantime, we can work hard and prepare ourselves for life's tests. We can do and give our best on a daily basis. Once we have done our best, we must learn to let go, to trust in a positive outcome, and to leave things in the hands of our Higher Power who accompanies each of us on our road through life. Learning to detach ourselves from the outcome of an event once we have done everything we can helps us to preserve useful energy and to confront new challenges.

☐ **Breaking Free**

Dora was eager to break out of the restrictive environment of her traditional Indian family. She was working as a nurse, and she was looking for the best opportunity to escape from her repressive home.

Her parents did not want her to mingle with the expatriates her girlfriends went out with, and they would have loved to see her married to a traditional Indian boy in Singapore. Dora had other plans, and she was willing to risk everything to make them come true.

Into the picture came Jason, half Australian and half French, who worked as a construction engineer in Singapore. He met Dora, a wonderful dancer, for the first time in a pub under the Hyatt Hotel. They started to talk and to dance, and he forgot all about his wife and two children in Australia. His relationship with his wife hadn't been too good recently, and he started to like Dora. They kept meeting and began dating. Dora liked Jason, and this seemed to be a ticket to freedom.

Singapore is too small a place in which to keep a secret. Dora's relatives had seen the couple together, and the problems at home started. Dora's parents kept her at home, and she was beaten for seeing Jason and threatened with more violence if she would not end the relationship. The only way out would be for her to let go of Jason—or to convince him and her family of a marriage. Convincing Jason was not hard, but dealing with her family was very difficult. Dora's father could not accept that his daughter wanted to marry a foreigner, and more spanking, more cries, and more terror came her way.

Dora's mother finally managed to talk sense into her husband. She convinced him that because Jason was an expatriate with excellent earnings, he had the means to support their stubborn daughter. They realized that Dora's relationship with Jason could not be kept secret from the small circle of suitable boys and, therefore, that a traditional wedding in their own cultural circle could no longer be arranged. After three months, the crisis was over and the wedding was set. As soon as Jason's divorce was final, the wedding was celebrated in Singapore.

Who is the winner in that situation? Jason? He truly loved and adored his young, modern wife. He gave up his former family to be with her. They left Singapore and were based in India and, later, in Australia for his work. What Jason did not know was that Dora never loved him like he loved her.

What about Dora? She was infatuated by Jason and proud that the good-looking man had fallen in love with her so easily. She was content because he treated her royally and had helped her escape from her restrictive home. Initially she did care for him, but the interest quickly faded. One year into her marriage with Jason, she met another man and fell in love all over again, but she would not leave Jason. She felt that she had settled and that Jason, as nice as he is, was a means to an end.

They are still together today, and while Jason has become very introverted, Dora has become more and more outgoing.

➢ Shades of Hopelessness

We humans—women, children and men—have strong emotions. We have to go through moments and sometimes years of agony, hardship, and pain before we can look beyond survival and deal with feelings like love and compassion.

When we look beyond mere survival and behind the walls of isolation put up by modern society, we often discover terrifying feelings of hopelessness. Many of us fight daily for our survival on the job or in our homes. We are pressured by constant deadlines, profound loneliness, and an eternal, self-imposed need for *more* and *better*.

We are exposed to tough competition. At times it is bitter cold out there in the "real" world. With constant fear nagging us, we become more ruthless with colleagues, friends, and family members.

Within ourselves, our ethics tell us that success and image cannot ultimately make up for the loss of values like trust and respect. Success is not a substitute for human closeness and intimacy.

My business trips around the world gave me the opportunity to get in touch with myself. I was confronted with feelings of despair, hopelessness, and isolation when the first impact of a new city and the excitement of professional success diminished. To my surprise, many "high fliers" in the international business world admit to having similar feelings. They are well accepted and admired in society, but lonely inside.

Feelings of hopelessness, isolation, and boredom are sometimes accompanied by abuse of legal drugs such as alcohol as people try to forget the restlessness, the steady pain, and the worry about tomorrow's impending business problems.

Many of us do not have a private fallback such as a loving family nor strong emotional attachments such as with a few close friends. It is lonely at the top. With no other goal than to excel in the fast lane of business, many of us forget to cherish each day and to love ourselves.

The values of life, joy, and gratefulness are more strongly expressed in the close, intimate relationships of families and tribes in Third World and in developing nations than they are in modern, industrialized societies.

Threatened by the daily challenge of keeping alive and of feeding their families, they affirm their yes toward life simply by living day by day. I have visited China, a fast growing industrialized nation in the East, and have lived for many months in India, where the deep philosophical ideas and religious traditions of many individuals intrigued me. The truly poor greeted me with a smile, even a man without legs who was begging in the streets. They did not approach me with feelings of jealousy nor with fear of competition, but with openness and curiosity. They were willing to accept me and to learn about me.

I have seen entire families in India working and living in the granite mines, where little boys and girls start to work at the age of four. By the time they are eight, girls skillfully carry heavy rocks in straw baskets on their heads. Again, women carry the heaviest burden in Indian society, regardless of age. Families survive by selling coconuts or bananas to people in passing cars. Often, they wait at the dusty roadside for hours to sell their produce.

I loved to watch them, loved to watch the women of the village washing clothing in the river not far from the road, and I remember the children—some barely dressed and others in only nature's raiment—bathing in the same small dimple in the stream.

I remember the immense beauty of the landscape and the solid brownish-red color of the earth, a color I have never seen in any other country. India is a land of great blessings. Her traditions, culture, and heritage are strong, and she is rich in human tragedy.

Despite terrible living conditions and the cruel truth that most Indians will never have the chance to break free from their misery, people there keep their faith. Even though they are free to move to another village or to the city, they cannot escape from their material poverty.

One might think that these people would be devastated and that all reason for living would have vanished long ago. But quite to the contrary, the poorest of the poor can teach us a lesson about the beauty and joy of life, about the very meaning of existence, in the way they confront the challenges of each and every day.

More does not necessarily mean *better.* Nor does having more money, more prestige, more freedom, or more social liberty buy happiness, a carefree mind, or love. In fact, possessions often seem to be accompanied by a sense of hopelessness and isolation. The plagues of Western consumer society can be harder to overcome than poverty.

Seldom in the West do we encounter an inviting, warm glance; smiles have become rare and precious; and it takes a tragedy to arouse our compassion. These valuable gifts are easily available from the poor and sick in the Third World. Facing existence in the terrible misery in the streets of Calcutta requires the will to survive and the ability to say yes to life itself.

How long would we survive with our attitudes and our petty needs in the streets of Calcutta? One week, maybe two? I doubt any longer. If we do not rediscover the sense of life that can be found in sharing and loving with true empathy, if we do not alter our attitudes and value what makes us human, we will continue to fail in giving meaning to our lives. We will fail to obtain peace and harmony.

➤ My Way

Life has bestowed a different story upon everyone. Everyone has a different path to travel, and we each have to go it alone. I believe that our destination was chosen before we saw the light of the world; the sun was chosen to be our guide and to provide us with brightness and warmth along the way.

We are all born to fulfill a special purpose on Earth and, in keeping with our unique mission, blessings and talents have been given to us in order to complete our purpose. The ingredients for our special vocation and the abilities to acquire additional knowledge are within us from birth.

Some of us have obtained support from our families to develop these special traits early in childhood. Others might not have obtained that kind of nurturing assistance. However, we can all start today by searching for our inner selves. We can begin working today toward accomplishing our mission.

What do we like passionately? What is our hidden treasure, our secret talent? Thinking about that and working with the ingredients we already have, the ingredients we appreciate most in ourselves, help us to discover ourselves. Brush aside the opinion of others and trust in yourself.

Success comes in many ways and can be expressed in various forms and shades. Look at a "successful" nun like Mother Teresa, who credited everything she did to her love for Jesus. Her trust in Jesus and her dedication were combined with extraordinary drive, engagement, and persuasiveness. Whenever you put your heart into a venture, you have a positive and promising chance to achieve miraculous outcomes.

Mother Teresa rescued millions of people from death and starvation. She provided a nurturing home for children and a place where the poorest of the poor could live and die with dignity. The mission of a single, strong-minded woman changed the world forever.

Martin Luther King Jr., a black minister who was working peacefully toward equality for all races, lost his life for his belief but changed the world forever. Millions of examples of sportsmen, artists, and businessmen could be mentioned. What do all of these people have in common? All of them looked inside themselves, found their purpose, and devoted themselves to a positive mission that became the center of their lives.

A purpose in life is necessary to identify our individual goals, to find our road. By using our individual gifts step by step, we can visualize and realize our mission. Walking the talk is necessary because actions speak louder than words. Trust, belief, and effort are necessary, but we all can make a difference in life. We all yearn to make a difference to ourselves, to our loved ones, and to the world. We yearn for love and acceptance.

By recognizing and choosing our own way and our own field of responsibilities, we can fulfill our deepest needs and become peaceful and content. In order to see the broader picture and visualize the end result, we need to choose our battles wisely and conserve our energy. Life is a marathon, not a 100-meter dash or a 1,000-meter run. To achieve an end goal, patience and persistence are required. To turn visions into reality, we often have to start over again even if we find ourselves on roads that are narrow and dark.

There are no shortcuts. There were no shortcuts available to help Mother Teresa follow her vision and answer her internal call to a life in India among the poorest people in the world. She had to walk steadily along the entire way. From her Balkan upbringings, she left for Ireland to join the order of the Sisters of Loretto. She then voyaged around the world to India. She traveled alone, with only God as her companion. She had to master foreign languages and adapt to the incredibly difficult circumstances she had chosen for herself. She kept her life in balance because her belief was strong and she had faith in her decision to devote her life to Jesus. She maintained her faith without guarantees or material wealth.

She started alone, and slowly more and more young, dedicated women followed her. Her order of the Missionaries of Charity was built not in days but through years of constant hard work. The order expanded from India throughout the entire world, and Mother Teresa's devotion and work eventually brought her and her cause the Nobel Prize. She cared neither for the honor nor the personal recognition the Nobel Prize brought to her, but she solemnly valued the public attention the prize offered to her cause and appreciated the increased funds for the poor that could be gathered.

She met statesmen and leaders but never strayed from her purpose. She stayed on track. That extraordinary woman, tiny in stature, was a steady rock in the storm, a simple woman who lived only to fulfill her mission to make the world a better place. She was the most remarkable female humanitarian leader of the twentieth century. Success is not indicated by material wealth. On the contrary, when we focus on what is important instead of on making money, material wealth might come as a secondary bonus. In Mother Teresa's case, faith and conviction brought her an incredibly long way, and she made a difference to the world.

She is an extraordinary example to reflect upon and to draw strength from. We might not be born to feed the hungry, but what is our mission? We might not found a potent organization that reaches all over the world, but what are our dreams? Where do we want to make a difference? Where can we make a difference? What are our gifts and talents?

It is helpful to think about the transitory nature of life. Precious time is passing day by day. We will have to leave this existence one day. We should be aware of that and take our chances now. When we leave, our material possessions will not matter to us anymore. Our human accomplishments and our relationships will. Wouldn't we like to be remembered for our humanity toward people, for the difference we made in people's lives?

We do not have the chance to live life all over again. Life is *now,* and that means choosing our way and working with the gifts nature has given to us. Let us affirm life day by day.

☐ Moving On and Letting Go

On any given day, thoughts of long lost friends and forgotten relationships will enter our minds. We will wonder about ourselves: What did we think during those times and why did we do the things we did? It was all so long ago that we can hardly recall. We play those scenes over and over in our minds. We are no longer emotionally involved: We are free.

The former Mr. Right no longer seems perfect (he's

rather unattractive, actually). Back then, life was more difficult. We went through sorrow and pain, and we put up with things we now tell our friends we would never tolerate. We did fulfill our dreams, and yet we could not make them last.

From the distance given to us by the passage of time, we have found answers to the questions of our youth. We have learned to be grateful for what we have. We are at peace with many things that did or did not occur.

Today, we are actually relieved that those who left us behind in tears, in fact, did leave us. We have learned to forgive others and, even more importantly, to forgive ourselves. We had hard lessons to learn. The lessons had to be repeated over and over. What was holding us back? Why couldn't we move on?

When I was younger, I was horrified by the thought of being left alone, of being left behind. Time taught me that those who leave us behind and move on are simply not the right people for us. They are not worth our time or our tears. Whomever we met and whomever we were attracted to in our lives were reflections of our state of mind and perception during that particular period. They helped us to discover truths and to learn about ourselves. We needed to learn a particular lesson from each person who crossed our path. When we take the chance to grow and to learn, we can be grateful instead of resentful for these experiences.

When we are younger, we are insecure and we obey all the rules young women should respect. We are shy; so we try to be nice and complaisant. We are scared of talking facts. We are scared of talking about what we really think and how we really feel.

Later we realize that a relationship that isn't built on such facts is not real. A man who sees a woman only as an attractive possession to flaunt instead of appreciating her as his spiritual and intellectual partner is not looking for a true partner and doesn't deserve to find one. Women often feel victimized by their partners and by unrewarding relationships. We forget to realize that we are generally not forced into a relationship but choose to enter it. Therefore, as long as women continue to surrender their beliefs and enter voluntarily into relationships that are limited to board and bed, at the most Italian or French cuisine, we give ground for unrewarding relationships.

As we grow older, we should grow wiser in choosing our partners and our friends. As time goes by, a shift of values occurs. External superficialities are replaced by lasting internal qualities. Young girls and women need to realize that time should never be a factor and that their biological clock is not reason enough to get into or stay in a relationship that they do not want. We do not run out of time. In the long run, qualities such as devotion and genuine caring are a sounder foundation than everyday commodities—and those qualities are worth waiting for.

More and more young professionals seem to be completely in charge when they're "on the job" at their brilliant careers, but when it comes to private relationships, they are insecure. They are stuck in unrewarding relationships with partners who do not appreciate them.

Women are always compromising, accepting the other person's ways, and "mellowing out" when it comes to their own values and needs in a partnership. How sad for us! If we can set adequate standards and live up to the expectations of our jobs, shouldn't we also make sure that our inner values and expectations, such as reciprocal respect and love, are met in our private lives? But how?

Cherishing ourselves first and foremost as well as respecting ourselves as women with equal rights in a partnership will help us. Believe it or not, like attracts like. As long as we are sending ambiguous messages and signals, we are attracting ambiguous, indecisive partners. Once we are emotionally available, intellectually mature, and spiritually ready, once we do not play games anymore and are serious about ourselves, we will attract the same in a potential partner.

Being self-aware, we can learn to trust ourselves step by step. We know it's a wide, beautiful world out there. Listening to our inner voice, reflecting on life, and practicing self-love make us take our time before we commit.

Once we have learned that hurt results from unwise, rushed decisions, we understand that to love and respect ourselves, we mustn't give away our energy. We have to keep our positive energy for ourselves and give it only to the person who appreciates our time, our effort, and our love.

December 1999

☐ Self-Acceptance: We Are Worth What We Think We Are Worth

Sometimes it seems that there's no escape from having one of those days again. We trip over our slippers trying to get out of bed. On the way to the bathroom, we drop our coffee cup. When we finally reach the bathroom, we take that horrendous, never-ending look in the mirror and our faces seem to have become longer, wider, and puffier (no wonder after all those heavy lunches and dinners and the occasional glasses of wine or beer).

Our look seems to pierce deeply, even beneath the skin. More fatty tissue and wrinkles seem to mark our faces, the eye, mouth, and forehead area. And the T-zone: Gosh!

The beautician must be right: After 25, women go downhill (and not only their skin). Our cheeks are less rosy than usual or too rosy all of a sudden. Our eyes are small, and our noses appear very wide. Is this the same woman we admired in the mirror yesterday? If so, what has changed?

What has changed is our mood and our attitudes toward life and toward ourselves. Remember, yesterday we were jumping out of bed like an excited puppy and within 10 minutes, we had our shower and makeup done. We were ready to face the world and, more important, we were ready to face ourselves. The seemingly small eyes we hate today had character yesterday, and the small lines on our foreheads were special marks of the serious businesswoman. We women let our attitudes and moods influence and change our points of view too easily. On those bad mornings, we put on a very dark pair of glasses through which we perceive the world and ourselves as hopeless, while if we had chosen the pink pair of glasses, our happy mood would have given vigor and beauty to the world. Looking through the dark glasses of our bad mood, we cannot value and love ourselves. We become unworthy, and our achievements and everything else is degraded. Our lives become ugly and dull. We feel totally out of rhythm, and we ask ourselves why we were even born.

Actually, taking one minute for ourselves before we even get up helps. Let us spend one minute and decide which of the two pairs of glasses we shall wear each and every day. If there really is no way around the dark pair, let us face it. We all have good days and not such good days.

We all feel happy and not so happy. Let us try during those down days not to let our bad mood in the morning ruin the entire day.

We, not our moods, can take the lead in our lives. Let us surrender to the idea that it might not be our best day—but we had a lot of good days already, didn't we? Doesn't this hard moment remind us how beautiful life is on the good days? Let us surrender to the fact that today we might not have accomplished as many things as we would have wished, but let us remember that soon we will be wearing our bright glasses again. Then, as has been the case so many times before, we will excel. We will achieve more than we planned. Patience and self-love are the important assets that get us through our dark days.

Why do we push ourselves so hard? We have fallen over our slippers and spilled a cup of coffee, that's all. We find ourselves less attractive today but, if we take a closer look beyond the dark glasses, we see that nothing has really changed. We are still ourselves, the loving partner, the caring friend, the attractive woman with all her positive qualities. We all look better on some days and less attractive on others—we do not have to let it get to us. We can accept it. Actually, we can be happy and grateful for those dark mornings. They help us live the happy days with more awareness and more gratefulness. They help us to embrace beautiful days as gifts.

We are worth what we think we are worth. We convey the impression of ourselves to others in how we act, talk, and behave. The real us will ultimately shine through.

In order to be patient and loving toward others, we must treasure ourselves first. The biggest favor we can do for ourselves and the most important gift we can give to ourselves is to learn to master our moods and to view them as temporary colorations, temporary perceptions of our lives.

December 1999

☐ One Step at a Time

This great lesson started out with a promise, a promise I made to myself at the beginning of 1999. It has taken me long years and enormous courage and setbacks to understand that I have to cherish and love myself first in order to love someone else. Loving myself enables me to receive the best kind of love from a nurturing and honest partner.

This knowledge came my way from 1996 to 1999, years I spent in Singapore, which was my self-chosen home, and which was where I found my best friend ever: Siew Ling. She has seen me through a lot of changes, and when I left Singapore in April 1999 (not by choice but because of the economic crises of Southeast Asia and my own financial miscalculations), I made a vow to come back.

I left for India, and the first weeks in Chennai (Madras) were hard. I was acquainted with India, especially the southern part of the country, but I grieved for the losses I had to bear from leaving Singapore and my best friend behind.

I was suffering from loneliness, as every single person sometimes does, but I was working in a fulfilling job. As a marketing consultant, I was responsible for building up the South American markets of an Indian granite company, and I was preparing for my first trip to Venezuela, Brazil, Chile, and Argentina.

The promise I made to myself was to find a very special person to share my life with. I saw myself faced with an enormous challenge. The first decision necessary in reaching a goal is to have a firm mind-set. With a firm, yet open-minded decision guiding us, we are able to move in the right direction and to refrain from second guessing ourselves all the time. I had learned over the years that having a goal does not mean achieving it immediately and at any cost. I had learned patience and endurance. I was not out to get myself a man. On the contrary, I felt ready, for the first time—if I were to meet the right person—to enter into a relationship, to share my life with a true companion and a partner.

To a certain degree, we are the masters of our fate. We set time frames and boundaries; we make sacrifices to reach a long-term goal. We need not be desperate. There is abundance in the world, enough for everybody to succeed and to be happy. I believe that whatever is meant for us will ultimately come to us and be ours. No one can ever take our blessings away.

So finally, I met Tom on June 19, 1999, at a romantic beach resort called Fisherman's Cove, 20 miles south of Chennai (Madras), the capital of India's largest southern state, Tamil Nadu.

I had just returned to the headquarters of my company from a five-week South American trip. Exhaustion and the need for solitude overwhelmed me, so I retreated for a week to the nearest beach resort. There, on a Saturday afternoon, I met my future husband.

As if in a fairy tale, a 6-foot, 4-inch tall, attractive prince with dark, silky skin who came from a faraway kingdom appeared before a princess at the beach. But I already knew that Cinderella was just an invention, and I really did not want to be "rescued" and then told the next day that all good times must sooner or later come to an end. No, thank you.

So I watched with big, untrusting eyes and learned that this stranger was an American engineer giving training sessions in India. It was refreshing that he had some manners and was interesting to talk to.

Based on my inner feelings and not on any ache of loneliness in my stomach, I agreed to join Tom for a drink. Later, we had dinner at the beach together with two of his senior colleagues. We spent an interesting evening discussing India, and I was even able to get some insight into the United States, a country I had never visited before. Tom was a truly self-accepting and self-aware individual, qualities that distinguished him from many businessmen and world travelers I had met before.

Well, in the end, I kept my promise. With her head squarely set on her shoulders and with her focus on her values and interior qualities, a woman can identify and choose the right man.

☐ **Quiet Time**

Grant yourself the pleasure of some quietness each day. Set aside time all for yourself. Confronted by the demands of our houses, our jobs, our families, and our children, we often forget about ourselves. The more loving and gentle we are with ourselves, the more understanding and caring we can act toward our loved ones.

We need to step back from life for at least a moment each day in order to distinguish between things that are important to us and things that the demanding roller coaster of business and society tells us are valuable. Our major investments of time, concern, and energy should never be wasted on things of minor importance.

But how do you make that distinction? Listen to your heart and soul every day for at least 20 minutes. Listen, relax, and let your thoughts flow: The answers will come.

➤ The Hunt

Kathy is a professional hunter. She hunts for love, emotional security, and to have a man in her life: a man who wants to commit to her, to love and treasure her for the rest of her life. She is an SPG, which means a Singapore Party Girl, hunting for an expatriate with a good position and salary in Singapore. In fact, what we are talking about is the seven "Cs": Club, Car, Cash, Credit Card, Comfort, Condominium and Cock. A lasting relationship and marriage are strongly preferred.

Kathy has been hunting for quite some time. Ten years have passed, and she has been left behind with a broken heart several times. Apart from her physical attractiveness, with her long, dark hair, brown eyes, and olive skin, she is a great singer. Her voice is as promising as Whitney Houston's. Kathy is a great singer and likes to perform at our friends' weddings—always the bridesmaid, never the bride.

I always pushed her to make more of her talent, to sing and to try for a recording contract, all that, but nothing happened. So I learned that changes can occur only if someone wants to change.

Actually, she used to go out with a friend of ours, an Irish banker, a good guy, but who was basically too boring for Kathy. To be fair to her, at that time she was still emotionally involved with her ex-boyfriend, a young English lad whose main attraction was a good body.

Kathy's relationships always ended, then another one started again shortly—and so it went, one relationship after the other. She was afraid to stay alone. She rushed into new relationships, and she gave of herself too quickly. She was too trusting, only to find out after a month or so that this was not "the one" or that he did not want to move as fast as she did, or that he was not available for a long-term relationship.

Actually, Kathy is hurting. Her father died when she was young, and as a beautiful young girl of Chinese-Indian descent, she did not feel very secure as she was growing up. She gets desperate whenever she is alone and she always dreamed of a better world where Prince Charming would rescue her from the constrained environment of the island of Singapore. She has big dreams of going to Europe or Hong Kong, but she never leaves Singapore. She works as an accountant from eight to five, all the while wanting to leave her job but never doing so.

She could have it all by working with her voice. Her singing was the most extraordinary I'd ever heard, but all she does is put her energy and her hopes into a never-ending cycle of new relationships with one man after another.

Some of the relationships were serious. In those cases, she drove each man away in turn with her crazy behavior or by flirting too intensely with someone else after a few drinks. She needed a lot of attention.

What she was really searching for was love, but what

she was failing to search for was a way to love herself first. I haven't seen Kathy for over a year, but I got the news that she is getting married in June 2000. I am very happy for her. I hope it will work out, and I hope she has finally learned to love herself.

May 2000

☐ The Lighthouse Perspective

From a distance, things always look so different. Imagine yourself standing on the Eiffel Tower in Paris, on the leaning Tower of Pisa in Italy, or on the 55th floor of a building on Park Avenue in New York City. Walking along the Great Wall of China taught me that detaching ourselves from our immediate circumstances helps us to see the bigger picture. It helps us to see things from a different angle, a different perspective.

Watching the world and seeing ourselves from a distance is spectacular. We see little men and women on their mobile phones, always rushing, always talking and negotiating, rushing along, checking things off from their tiny to-do lists in their day planners.

Viewing us, a spectator might ask himself: "Do these earthlings ever stop as they rush along, even for the shortest moment?" If people did stop, they would recognize that harmful activities and choices consume their lives, day and night. Why would they need to have constant reminders and carry electronic organizers for keeping track of the truly important human matters like love and compassion? They could just as well carry them in their hearts and souls, just as they could carry the love for their partners. But where have the feelings gone? Just as the memories of a sunny afternoon's swim or a peaceful walk in a wintry park become unaffordable, replaced by the overrated urgency of tax reports and never-ending meetings with future business partners, so too do we become too busy to feel.

Distance is needed in order to return to the simple but important things in life. Detachment and time are needed in order to discover what is right and truly meaningful to us.

☐ Courage

It takes courage to get up every morning, to face the challenges of another day. We are educated at an early age to be brilliant actors on the stage of life. We learn quickly to play all the required roles; soon we excel. The more roles we master—mother and partner, chairwoman and social friend, daughter and lover—the busier and more interesting we become.

The busier we are, the more success we have, or so one is tempted to believe. Many of us have fallen for and accepted this idea as unquestionably true.

But this is a misconception and a wrong interpretation of courage. True success requires true courage. Let us take off our masks and show our true beliefs and values. Let us stop acting! We might then know, for the first time, what courage means when we confront our true selves. We are actually so different on the inside from what we project every day to the world.

To stop acting is easier said than done. It requires courage to accept our individuality and, as a consequence, to accept ourselves for who we are. Discovering ourselves is one thing, while daring to show ourselves to others and to stand up for our beliefs is another. It can get very lonely out there, but remember that true friends will remain.

☐ **Quality, Not Quantity**

When we start to search for harmony and peace inside of ourselves and when we discover who and what truly matters to us, then we will have fewer roles to play. We might lose touch with acquaintances and friends who cannot accept our new value system and outspokenness. When we learn to dedicate our time to ourselves and people who enrich our lives and promote our growth, we might expect fewer "spectacular" events and less "excitement" from life. We will start to focus on the quality of life: quality time spent with people we care for, fewer meetings but more definite outcomes, and a focus on solutions instead of on problems.

I remember years ago when I loved to party with a crowd, sometimes all night long, and every night I enjoyed too much wine. I also remember the days after when I had a headache and no one to turn to. Today, I still love to party and to dance once in a while with my circle of friends, and I still enjoy a fine dinner, a glass of good wine, and an engaging conversation, but none of it needs to be so loud or intense.

The day after, my friends and I will happily chat over the phone about our pleasant, rewarding evening, and we will reflect on our gathering with true people of the real world instead of on a stage play. The night will not have left any traces of pain or guilt in our heads. Less has become more.

When we have learned to set our priorities, we are able to choose the important over the unimportant and to prevent our days and our lives from getting out of control.

Part 2

THE GUIDING MOON

"The moon, shining in the darkest of nights,

confirms that darkness can never prevail,

never exist without light.

At the end of the darkest of nights,

there is brightness and light.

Continue on your path.

Confront the darkest of life's challenges

and let the moon guide you through the night

to find the light of the day." (D.S.)

The rain has finally stopped, but we can still feel the cold wind blowing. We can still feel the last traces of the freezing rain on our skin, and we shiver inside. The night sets in. We are comforted as the darkness protects us from curious eyes, but we are scared because we cannot yet distinguish what threatens us with harm from the healthy, vital goodness that is waiting for us. We are struggling with ourselves.

We are still trying to win the one fight we can never win: the struggle against ourselves. In the dark of the night, we ask ourselves what we did wrong and why life seems so unmanageable at times. The darkness brings the fears of our childhood to life: fear of confronting the world and fear of discovering ourselves. The night covers us with a blanket of guilt, guilt for having thought, done, and said things long ago, for having inflicted pain on others, for having messed up, and for having not lived up to our own very high standards.

Engrossed in our thoughts, we can suddenly find light shining through, shining upon us, a light that brings hope and brightness from the dark sky: the moon. The faraway orb consoles us and brings brightness to the black night. It returns time and again to lighten the darkness and the feelings of despair in our lives. Frequently it comes to us not as the moon itself, but in the form of a loving heart, a helping hand, or an understanding person.

Let us hold on to it. Don't let it go. It helps us to focus on the brightness of life, to forgive others and ourselves and to keep walking until we can overcome a difficult passage on the road of life.

The path will lead us out of the dark valley and bring us more harmony and contentment, eventually taking us along the passage to the top of the mountain. The path is paved with blessings, and no one can hold us back if we follow the light. Facing the difficult and painful experiences of life leads us ultimately out of the valley.

After learning the basic lessons of life, the deepest of all valleys can be crossed. As we walk through the night, the moon guides us on the first passage to climb the mountain. The bridges we have to cross are many, but looking back, we realize that we have come a long way since the beginning of our journey.

Now, to fully discover our hidden treasure, we must trust in our Higher Power and deepen the trust in ourselves. We remember that all difficulties along the way are merely exercises and tests. We have the capability and strength to pass them.

By perceiving life as the greatest professional school that exists, we can appreciate that the attendance is free with no strings attached and no material investment required. As in any other school, we must devote our full attention to our studies in order to succeed.

Life's lessons are free. Can you imagine the tuition at the Institute of Life? Honestly, I can't, but I am sure no one would be able to afford it, which is to say that life is not as unfair as many of us think it is.

➢ My Hero

Sue was born the youngest of 10 children to African American parents in southern Mississippi. By the time she was 1, her parents left their farm in the country to move to the city. Sue was a very active and fun-loving child. She loved to play in the water, especially the laundry water, and was known as "Joy Bleach" by her family members.

By the age of 7, Sue faced increasing problems with her eyesight. She could not see properly in the dark, and she stumbled into things and fell over objects she could not see. By the age of 15, her field of vision had been reduced by half. A diagnosis was made, but the medical term for Sue's disease was discovered only much later, retinitis pigmentosa (RP), a disease with no cure. The initial symptoms of the most common type of RP are problems moving in the dark, which is eventually followed by total night blindness and a gradual reduction in the field of vision. This explains Sue's stumbling into things. A normal person sees beyond the distant point on which the eyes are fixed, but a person with RP loses this ability. Many people with RP behave during daylight and in familiar environments the same way people with normal vision do. In darkness or in rapidly changing light conditions, however, they behave almost as blind people do.

I met Sue for the first time in 1999 in Chicago, where she continued to share an apartment with her mother. At 44, she worked as an office manager for the U.S. government in downtown Chicago. Despite the initial worries of her family, she attended a regular high school, and only in her last year of college did she transfer to the Lighthouse for the Blind to complete her education. Since Sue can move about very confidently, especially in familiar territory, she often makes us forget about her disease. She can catch the bus every morning and, if you were to meet her along the way, you would probably not be able to tell that she is nearly blind. She has always been a helpful, popular colleague and a warm friend. She is in love with life and has learned to live with her disease.

During one of our lunch dates, Sue told me about Chicago and, while we crossed Madison Street to the Presidential Towers, said she wanted to take me to Marina Bay in the evening. When we entered the dim light of a Chinese restaurant, Sue reached for my hand. It took me a moment to understand that her eyes could not adapt to the dim light, that she could not see in the darkness.

Sue is a person who believes wholeheartedly in the beauty of life. She knows that there is no cure for her disease and that she can hope only that her field of vision does not deteriorate any further. I have never heard her complain. She is a happy, proud woman and values the little things in life more than many of us do. She loves to dance, and she goes swimming twice a week with friends. Her passions include movies and the theater, and her vision problems have not caused her to give up on her passion. She watches videotapes at home more than she does movies in theaters, and she is still an expert on films. RP is a strange disease, and we cannot understand nor foresee its course. While Sue has learned to trust and to accept that there is no cure, she proclaims her acceptance of a new way of life. To Sue, life is a gift, and seeing even as little as she does is a daily gift. Sue is a very strong and special woman, and she is my personal hero.

☐ Being Human

Not long after visiting the United States for the first time, I encountered a most remarkable experience of human frailty. It made me reflect on how often we humans act inhumanely, hurt ourselves, insult people, and discriminate against others because they are apparently different from us—but are they really? Acceptance, tolerance, and empathy in the face of difference are among the most important values in life; unfortunately, they still are not a priority for many members of modern society.

It was Sunday, November 21, 1999, and I was on an afternoon flight from Miami to Dallas when life put me through a disturbing test. We were coming home from the Bahamas, and we had left Nassau in the late morning and arrived on time in Miami to board the connecting flight to Dallas.

We shouldn't have been in such a hurry. The flight was delayed for two hours. As we waited in line for our boarding passes, we laughed because only a while before, such a delay could have ruined my day. I would have allowed myself to get angry. The fear of not making it for a scheduled meeting on a timely connecting flight would have taken over and disturbed my peace of mind.

Those stressful and harmful times were gone. During the previous few years, I had experienced hours upon hours of waiting, especially in India where flights were routinely delayed or canceled when bad weather conditions or technical problems did not allow for a timely departure.

The reality is that the most importance should be given to the safety of passengers and the crew. What does it matter if we arrive two or three hours late to a meeting when the other alternative could be death?

I like the idea "Death is the opposite of time." If we adhere to this maxim, then schedules and meetings won't mean anything to us and full calendars and overflowing desks won't haunt us because we will have given up emphasizing the cycles of worldly activities.

It is hard to understand, for instance, why people on board airplanes jeopardize the safety of so many passengers with "important" calls on their cell phones. It has been reported that at least 35 percent of cell phones and pagers on board planes are not turned off when people are requested to do so before flights take off and upwards of 65 percent of the devices are turned back on long before disembarkation. People want to make sure they catch the latest update. I would bet that seldom are these calls made to family members or friends; instead, people are hunting for business and new opportunities in order to make more money.

It is sad to see how our business agendas dictate our availability for joy and relaxation and, ultimately, for participation in our own lives. Shouldn't we make use of time and stop letting time control us? Where is our ability to make healthy judgments?

When we made it to the ticket counter during our delay in Miami, we received word that the scheduling situation was awful. Even though we had purchased adjoining seats, we could not be seated together. We did obtain two aisle seats in opposing rows, but holding a conversation would not be possible. The attendant at the counter was friendly, and our best option was peaceful acceptance of the unfortunate situation.

But then our reception on board the airplane was extremely cold. Not long into the flight, I was subjected to an incident of discrimination over race and national origin, which was further complicated by a flight attendant. This display of prejudice and aggression particularly struck me as it happened in the United States: Mr. Frederick, a flight attendant, refused to give available seats to my partner and me because we are an interracial couple. Tom was addressed as "a person like you," and before we left the aircraft, the same attendant who had used those words called us "trash" in front of the captains and main stewardess. He also informed us that they did not need people like us on their airline. The other stewardess and the captains were shocked and offered us champagne. This was totally inappropriate and out of line. I spent many hours writing in order to bring this incident to the attention of the airline authorities, without result: They did not ever reply to our complaint.

I had been taught that America and her inhabitants form a melting pot of different races of people with various beliefs and that people whose origins are in different cultures would be treated the same. To me, America was a country that proclaimed hope and freedom and offered a sheltering home for the victims of persecution. The Statue of Liberty seemed to me an eternal symbol of a country that fought worldwide racial, religious, and national discrimination, a country that supported Third World nations with food and other help.

During my first visit to Chicago, a Greek immigrant from Athens had strengthened my belief. Her simple philosophy was explained in heavily accented English: "Sweetheart, don't you worry. My accent and your accent are fine here anyway. No one is American. We are all from different places, all immigrants."

I thought America would be filled with so many people who had arrived there and were still dreaming of a land of liberty and peace. For centuries, people have borne heavy burdens to reach the country of unlimited possibilities. And they still do: Just look at the enormous waves of refugees from Cuba and China.

Wouldn't anyone try to escape from a reality as tough as theirs? They believed that in America—the sunshine after a long rain—their dreams could come true at the end of the rainbow. My trust in that relevant truth was shaken by our experience on that flight to Dallas, and I have remained untrusting toward America's stand on the principles of equal rights for all races.

The airline episode filled me first with hostile anger, then with sadness, and finally with the wise knowledge that we humans carry both the very best and the very worst inside of us. It is up to each individual to choose the good over the bad, the fair over the unfair, and love over hate.

The more challenging experiences we overcome and the more tests we pass in our lives, the more accepting we become. Unfortunately, some of us never do learn to love ourselves or to address our inner issues. This is what keeps us from loving and accepting others and knowing that, independent of race, color, or nationality, we are all human. When we understand how much we can learn from different cultures and races, it opens our minds. Our inner thoughts and beliefs can bring either grace and blessings or hurt and sadness to mankind. Our beauty is within us and is not a reflection of our language, appearance, or skin color.

After our experience on that flight, I jotted down my reflections, and I wondered if we all don't have a little of that flight attendant in us.

Even if we have traveled the entire world, we have never truly traveled to our inner self. No plane can bring us there, and no leader can show us the way. It is a long and lonely trip to take, and along the way, we will discover many things we do not like and appreciate about ourselves. It is necessary to be frank with ourselves, so let's not lie: There is nothing to gain but much to lose.

All too often, we hold others responsible for our reactions and our behavior, but the truth is that we do have choices. We might not like our jobs—we can leave them. We might not love ourselves—let us deal with it.

Let us find a starting point, and we will discover some good within us. We might have racial prejudice—let us ask ourselves why. Don't each of us belong to some minority that fights against discrimination? Let's think for a while, and we will find that if we do not always take ourselves so seriously our priorities will change.

When we change our attitudes and thinking patterns, we will change. We will become kinder to others and to ourselves. Self-acceptance and self-awareness are the first steps on the long journey toward our true home, toward ourselves.

Maybe we have had a bad day. We might be tired from a long day's work, a long flight, or a troublesome personal situation, but does it help to act out and insult others? Compassion and forgiveness set our souls and minds free for the most important thing: *life*. We all need to ask ourselves about the sources of aggression and racial hatred.

Why do we feel intimidated when a person of a different race is asking for our assistance? Is it because we are afraid of the unfamiliar? Is there actually any difference between us? Where did our parents come from that we proudly call ourselves American citizens: Europe, Asia, Africa? Doesn't this beautiful planet belong to all of us?

Do we often use racial difference as an excuse for aggression? Which of our aims can we achieve, which of our desires can we fulfill with unworthy means? Do we believe that having power over people will bring us satisfaction or take away the helplessness and powerlessness we feel inside?

Does threatening people make us feel important and potent for the very moment? Don't we realize that this feeling vanishes within seconds and leaves us emptier than before? Empty inside?

Does calling people liars and "trash" because they are different in race, color, religion, or nationality take away our anger at mankind? Does our hate for different races quench the thirst for self-acceptance in our hearts?

Hating, insulting, and nonacceptance can never satisfy the thirst for love, satisfaction, and acceptance. How long will it take us to learn this?

Provoking and stereotyping others and commenting on "different" individuals or on minorities cannot help us feel better about ourselves. On the contrary, once we utter words of hate, we start to feel a loss of energy inside. Engaging in racial discrimination and hate violates the basic principles of being human. It does not qualify us for our jobs. Worse, it does not qualify us for life.

None of us is free from prejudices that are caused by our fear of the unknown, of new situations, and of people with different cultural backgrounds. However, we need to realize that the world belongs to all of us. There is abundant space for all heritages and cultures, and we can live together in acceptance and understanding. Otherwise, the suffering of our ancestors to find peace and equality was in vain.

Destruction, killing, and hurt will continue until we learn our lessons. Because of jealousy and fear, we kill the love of our partners. Because of a lack of acceptance that causes hate, we kill the spirit of the people who are different than us. Compassion and understanding are ways to love. And love means victory.

➢ Prejudice and Perception

In order to perceive situations objectively, it is necessary for people to be self-secure and to have well-developed values. Generally, we try to perceive reality and to reflect on events in a way that makes them fit into our life and our world picture.

We easily forget that the world is made up of different kinds of people, all with different agendas and unique minds. This fact is hard to accept for most of us. It starts in the family. We take sides with people of our own gender, race, and religion in questions of life and death as well as in daily situations at our workplace or even on shopping tours. We take sides and make judgments before we evaluate what a situation is truly like.

Sometimes we are not even aware of a problem, but we are already busy judging people and their behavior. We seem to know what our partner thinks and what is right for him. We seem to have all of the information we need already fully formed in our minds; we think, act, choose, and decide for everyone.

It does not work out. Communication does not work when we shape what the other party says to fit into our world picture. We must learn that a preconceived picture does not reflect reality. Our preconceived opinion does not give others a chance to be themselves. We label them before they can express what they need to say and what they mean. We use labels such as good, bad, black, white, European, African, Asian, Christian, Buddhist, wrong, right. What we forget is that we are all unique human beings. We are beautifully colored personalities with various strengths and weaknesses. No one fits in the category of a black-and-white world picture. Isn't the world interesting and challenging because we are all different? Isn't the world beautiful and colorful because we complement each other?

Self-aware people are able to step back and get perspective on life. It helps them to see the world more objectively. They have learned to listen, and they do not judge.

There are fine shades of gray within the black-and-white image of our world idea. Nothing is right or wrong unless it starts with a thought. We create battles in our heads, and we fight them in the streets. Insecurity and fear form our judgmental attitudes toward our fellow beings.

Our inability to let a situation evolve naturally before us and to detach ourselves from assuming things about what we think are obvious facts makes us believe that everybody and everything has to fit our world picture in order to make us happy. How often do we comment on events that we did not witness? We allow racial insult and discrimination to go unnoticed and unacknowledged as long as they do not hurt our own interests and the interests of our social circle.

Thinking back on the racial discrimination my black partner experienced on the aircraft, it is clear that not only was he exposed to the discriminating remarks of a single flight attendant, but he also encountered something more painful: a judgmental group of passengers who by their inaction were taking sides with a member of their own ethnic group. They unconsciously protected a white male, who was a member that "belonged" to their group. Sad, isn't it? Shouldn't justice come before color and race?

I wonder how they would react if they saw the same person come into their office the next day, maybe as their new colleague or their new boss. The fact is that we have choices in life; we can choose our attitudes and direct our minds. Our thoughts and actions are not only biologically determined, for we are also people with free wills.

Often we try to protect someone of our own group even though he or she has committed a wrong. The wrong never becomes right even if a thousand people proclaim it to be so. The courage to be different—to point out to a loved one or a member of our group that he or she did not act rightly or to confront a situation with a truly objective approach—can cost us our place in society.

The starting point is within our own hearts and our own lives. Looking inside ourselves and thinking before we act helps us not to judge others presumptuously. Evaluation and analysis are important. Our own views are valid for us only; they may never be generalized to all situations or all people. They are only a small part of a bigger picture.

➤ Slipped Back

On our journey through the school of life, we face many setbacks. They often occur when we believe we have finally mastered a lesson, our moods, or an old behavior pattern.

When that happens, it is painful to admit that we have lost our temper again over the same issue with the same person. It is much easier to find excuses and to blame circumstances, life, and other people instead of assuming our own responsibility. A part of growth is accepting our responsibility and realizing that we are not perfect. We need to admit our errors to ourselves. Then we won't allow setbacks to make us feel guilty and hopeless, for we know the same lesson will be repeated again until we master, understand, and control our reactions.

It is not necessary to beat ourselves up, to feel shame, and to blame ourselves. Let's just accept the fact that we have to try again next time and let it go.

➤ Relaxation in Industrialized Style

While flipping through the newspapers, surfing the Internet, or switching on the TV, often we are using technological advancements to escape from loneliness and painful realities. For women, shopping is a common diversion. We shop in order to run from our lives; and we are spending our money to avoid sitting down and reflecting upon ourselves. Spending time alone frightens most of us. Even single people who are living by themselves often avoid actually being alone.

Most families constantly listen to the radio, and the TV is always on—a connection to the outer world. What is it that makes us want to avoid the inner world and inner awareness? Our agendas are filled with meetings, dinner appointments, bar stops, or shopping tours. We try to avoid our own company. We desperately need to be "out there," in the company of others.

How many of us have taken the time to write a life analysis, to reflect on what we want for ourselves and what we already have, to think about who we are and what we would like to be in the future? Activities like that help us to obtain self-awareness and, if necessary, to change our direction and to get back on track. How many of us keep a diary to share our most intimate thoughts?

Listening to commercials and seeing the store shelves

overflowing with items we will never use, I sometimes wonder if the daily shopping list of many of us truly looks like the following:

I am scared—I will buy a gun that will protect me, that will make me feel safe and secure. No one can harm me anymore.

I am feeling depressed—I will get myself some of those "happy pills" I took last time.

I believe I can fly—I will get myself some crack, and I will be sure I can fly.

I am feeling empty inside, and I am unconnected with myself—I will get myself good and drunk, and I will definitely forget about all of that.

I am feeling lonely in the middle of a thousand people—I will meet up with my buddies and have a night out, dancing, screaming, getting high. I might not come home until the next morning at 5 a.m., but I won't feel lonely anymore.

I am aware that I need some romance and love in my life—I will switch on the TV, and there it will be.

I need some action—I will rent the latest action thriller, and I will have what I need.

I long for a nice meal in a comfortable place to nurture my soul and body—I will grab a quick burger and chips, I will no longer be hungry.

I need a friend—I will buy myself a diamond or eat as much chocolate as I want.

I am sad—I will buy one of those expensive new outfits that will make me happy.

I am tired—I will just take some headache medicine or drink a Red Bull, and that will get me through the day and solve my problems.

But does all of this bring happiness or does it bring despair? Are our problems really solved by such means or are we just looking for a quick fix? Shortcuts are "in," and no one seems to take the time anymore to walk the entire length of their journey.

Are we confronting the challenges of life? Are we willing to go deeper and to learn about ourselves? Our *self* is all each of has in the end. It is a frightening thought for most of us, and we try to avoid the "road less traveled" that brings us back home.

Alcohol and other drugs and crime committed with guns all have one thing in common: They never bring solutions, healing, or hope. In the end, such activities will cause our account to be overdrawn. Our debits will soon be big enough for everyone to notice: our boss, our clients, our family, our friends, and at the very end, ourselves. Our misery often has to become intolerable before we will accept change.

It is our choice to modify our "shopping lists" and to find real remedies. Consider the following:

I am scared—If I buy a gun that will protect me and make me feel safe and secure, aren't I becoming part of the weapon-selling network? Wouldn't it be better to try to deal with my fear? Can I try to discover, by getting in touch with myself, why I am afraid and what I am truly scared of?

I am feeling depressed—If I get myself some of those "happy" pills, won't I be passing that kind of behavior on to my children and friends. Shouldn't I find the courage to face the truth and the causes of my despair?

I believe I can fly—If I get myself some crack, won't I be supporting the drug dealers as they lure me to use their "enjoyable" drugs. Wouldn't it work for me to realize that I can "fly" by achieving my goals and by believing in my

Higher Power and myself?

I am feeling empty inside, and I have lost touch with myself—If I drink and smoke enough to forget about it all, aren't I risking addiction to alcohol and nicotine? Aren't I mistakenly escaping from myself by destroying my liver and lungs and, at the same time, financing the alcohol and cigarette industries? Instead, can I try to understand the emptiness inside of me and try to reestablish the bond with myself? Do I appreciate the gifts I can bring to mankind? Am I actually aware of myself?

I am feeling lonely in the middle of a thousand people— If I meet up with my buddies and have a late night out, isn't it a problem that work will begin at 8 a.m., a few hours after the partying is over? Can't I strive to feel complete with myself and surround myself with healthier friends who nurture themselves and our friendship? Nurturing ourselves means listening to our own needs, the needs of our unique bodies for healthy food, exercise, and enough sleep. A good night's sleep makes the new day a different, more positive experience. Cherish the day, for each new day offers a new start, a new learning experience in our short journey through time. Every day is precious, too precious for us to be feeling overwhelmed by tiredness and hangovers.

I need some romance and love in my life—If I switch on the TV to find it, aren't I using my time on Earth merely to watch instead of to live life and to love? Can't I see that watching can't ever be enough for us? We are beautiful beings with insight and intelligence. We hold the power to choose what is happening in our lives. We can overcome difficulties.

I need some action—If I just go get the latest action thriller, aren't I misunderstanding what true action is? The word *action* is derived from the word *act*. To act means to get our butts up and discover the world and its wide possibilities. No film will ever give us the excitement we can experience in true life. Day in and day out, life is better, more unpredictable, and more challenging than any action film has ever been. We are living in the real world and not in the world of make-believe.

I long for a nice meal in a comfortable place to nurture my soul and body—If I just get a quick burger and chips to satisfy my hunger, doesn't the burger take only the immediate feeling of hunger away but not the thirst for a comforting homemade dinner in a nurturing environment?

I am sad and need a friend—If I buy myself a diamond (or an expensive new outfit or all the chocolate I can eat) to make myself happy, don't I realize that the happiness over my newly found "friend" won't last even until we are home? We can wear it or eat it, but it can't hold us when we need a hug, listen to our pain, or share our joy. It is just another toy that will end up forgotten in the closet or jewelry box. And the pounds we gain from eating chocolate are not easily left behind, so we often must carry them for quite some time. Let us deal with our sadness. Where does it come from? We can reward ourselves for a hard day's work, but let us not confuse rewarding ourselves with acting out of desperation.

I am tired—If I just take some of those painkillers or drink some liquor to get me through the day, thinking my problem is solved, won't the cause of my headache remain? We can hide for a few hours behind a painkiller, but why not focus on some basic changes to get rid of the actual problem that causes our stress? Maybe it is long working hours, not enough sleep, or constraints put on a relationship? Let us talk to our inner selves and explore the reasons that cause our pain. We must start to address the problems, not the symptoms. Let us stop hurting ourselves.

➤ The Cinderella Complex

The title of Colette Dowling's book for women, *The Cinderella Complex,* always makes me think of my friend Christine. This is ironic because Christine is one of the few women I have met who has completely overcome the need to be rescued by Prince Charming. She got married about four years ago to an American engineer and moved from Singapore to California. She has learned to love the United States but still looks forward to her yearly trip home. Certainly it was not easy in the beginning. She and her husband met in Singapore shortly before Rick's assignment was over. He had to leave Asia and get back to work in the States. They had one month to get to know each other before he left. And he was leaving for good, or at least for a year. They kept in touch through e-mail, and their wedding was planned online. Even though Rick was a great guy, he was not, in fact, Christine's true love. Christine was a modern Singapore Indian. She was educated in Christian ways by her mum, and the divorce of her parents had taken place long before.

Christine had, with time, become practical. She had been in love with Andy, who was based in Singapore for a long time. Andy shared a flat with her but did not show serious intentions of staying. He was not yet thinking of his future. Christine thought of their future all the time. She was in love, but she also knew she wanted to get married and to have a family. She wanted a regular relationship and stability. Certainly there's nothing wrong with that! She was strong enough that when Andy left for overseas, she moved back to her mother's home. She made a decision to end a relationship because it had no future.

Shortly after that, she ran into Rick. Rick, a serious guy with a good head on his shoulders, fell in love immediately with the smart and attractive Singapore girl. Initially, Christine did not feel as intensely for Rick as he did for her, but she appreciated his honest concern and the security he offered. She felt safe with him.

When I last met Christine in Singapore, she had come there for a vacation. Rick was also in town. She seemed very content and told me she was learning to appreciate and love Rick more, day by day. Some say she has settled, but I believe she has done much more than settle. She is happy, and during a recent correspondence, I learned that she feels fulfilled and is pregnant with her first baby. Thank God, at least some of us have given up on the old belief that, to be true, love must cause pain.

➤ Things Are Not Always as They Seem

Sometimes love is not enough. We love our parents, we cherish our husbands, we adore our children, but our loved ones always leave. Our children seem to drift further and further away from us. While our spouse or partner is generally old enough to make adult decisions on his own, which we can question but not change, the situation with our children is difficult.

Persuaded by their role models and influenced by society and friends, at different stages of their lives our children have to be introduced and led toward life's new challenges and expectations. Introducing and guiding them is difficult at times, especially without taking over their lives and making decisions on their behalf.

While a newborn baby is like a fresh slate on which we can engrave our fundamental ideas of life and living, a nearly adult child has outgrown that approach to parenting. Our children will constantly face new situations and, as much as we wish to give them direction, well-meant advice is often not welcome.

It is expressing tough love when we stand back and watch, not helping out time and again when our almost-adult child is in financial trouble; it is tough love to mind our own business when we see someone we care for struggling. We know that there will be no change if we do not change our own behavior first. We would like to make life easier for our children, our sons and daughters. We would like them to enjoy their journey, their life. We would like to protect them from reality, from having to learn tough lessons.

To make our children healthy players in the game of life, we must allow them to have their own experiences, we must allow them to face the cold winds of reality. We must give them our best advice when asked for it, but then let them make their own decisions. Our job is to help them understand that life sooner or later will give back but also will take away. Let us allow them to learn that as adults they will be confronted with the consequences of their actions. We can help them face reality. They will be grateful, in the long run, for our tough love.

➤ Take a Minute: Thinking and Acting

In our fast-paced society, we hardly take time to reflect anymore. We react to situations, and thinking comes later. Why? Maybe because we think there is no time for reflection, that the people we're involved with will not wait for our reply because the situation needs immediate attention.

We are so used to acting that we often start to take action without leaning back to reflect upon what is really needed to solve a problem or to give the correct reply to a question. We hardly take time to read a report or a book completely. We find our eyes flying over documents, trying to accumulate the essential, but very often we miss out on what is most important.

In a book we read the last chapter first. And while our partners are talking to us, we are impatiently waiting for our turn to reply. Everything is rushed, and there is no time to reflect. We must react to a situation (this is what we believe) because we are afraid of losing the opportunity.

We have to learn that opportunities are seldom one-time events, that the truly important ones will return. We must realize that if a person or a situation does not grant us time to reflect, it might not be for us.

Taking time for reflection gives us the chance to see a situation objectively and to be aware of its potentially positive and negative effects. By reading and listening closely, without jumping to conclusions, it is possible for us to become better businesspeople, friends, and partners.

If we learn to stop and think before we act and if we don't allow ourselves to be rushed by people or circumstances, we will more successfully confront life's challenges.

➤ Quietness

Most of my Indian friends, independent of status and caste, reserve a small corner of their house or a small room for their prayers and spiritual exercises. They withdraw from the busy world to their special place to find quietness and calmness through prayer and reflection.

In Western society, I have hardly ever come across similar arrangements for daily meditation. We seem to have no extra time for our beliefs, for quietness, or for our higher spirit and ourselves.

We see our loved ones while rushing off to work or getting home from evening activities. How much do we really share? Or better yet, how much do we really want to share, to commit?

Often we do not know what another person means to us until it is too late; and we indefinitely delay important decisions that involve our private life. We are so busy running around that we neglect to reflect on what we are really about and what our life is really about.

Setting aside quiet time for ourselves every day helps us to become aware of what we are grateful for. Ultimately we will become more loving and gain deeper contentment that we can pass on to our families, friends, and even strangers. Ten to 20 minutes each day spent engaged in reading and reflection—spent solely in discussion with our higher spirit—can change our lives forever.

We make time and spend money for many superficial things, things that don't do us or others any good. As soon as we have bought some new item, we realize that it just takes up more space in our houses and our thoughts. Things merely cause us more worries because we have to keep paying for them.

I believe we all can make some special place for quiet time. First we make space in our mind, then in our day, and later maybe a special place in the outer world where we can sit on the floor and reflect and pray, where we can find ourselves. A harmonious atmosphere makes it easier to relax.

Most of us do not like looking into ourselves. Most of us seem to be afraid of extra time spent alone. Often we complain about boredom, but isn't it that we are afraid of being left to our very own thoughts?

Make space today for yourself. Light a candle and think about the beauty of your life and of living. If you don't see any beauty, imagine where you can find it and imagine it coming into your life. Enjoy your uniqueness in being human and reflect on the gift of life and the chances given to you—without expectations or strings attached. Nurture and love yourself. Treasure yourself by setting aside time every day to engage in reflection, meditation, and prayer.

➤ What Money Cannot Buy

Have you realized that the most beautiful things in life are free? A perfect sunset on a late summer evening, a walk in the forest or at the seaside, a smile from someone in the crowd, devotion and love of the poor who ask for nothing but acceptance, a consoling word to a sick friend, a helping hand for someone who is struggling, and time for family conversation and togetherness: Each is absolutely free.

Imagine that all of the above were missing in our lives but that our bank accounts were full. Would it really matter? Why do we still ask for more material wealth when we can't fulfill the purest of human endeavors: compassion?

December 27, 1999

➤ Other People's Lives

"Sweetheart you have not forgotten about it?"
"Forgotten about what?" I ask myself, smiling at Tom. It dawns on me—the company's Christmas party. In one of my weak moments, I had agreed to go. Not a big deal, just a reasonable decision because I know Tom would like to stop by. "Anyway, it won't be longer than three endless hours," I tell myself.

From the hottest outfit to the latest affair in the business world, other people's lives are discussed and put on display during such events. It is hard to avoid the "Did you hear this and that?" the "Look at them ..." and other such remarks during this kind of social meeting. In the past, I abused more than a couple of margaritas to get through such gatherings.

Older and wiser, I am now more relaxed and I can get through the hours more easily. If I can excuse myself, I avoid participating in the first place, but this time I had committed. I can hear myself answering for the ten thousandth time the same questions: "Where are you from?" "Where did you meet?" "Oh, what a different accent?" I know some of them mean well. My favorite answer would still be that I am from the moon, which would explain the accent as well. "I guess it would stop all further questions," I think while I am rushing to get dressed.

I always find it painful that it brings fulfillment to so many people to pay so much attention to the lives of their friends. They have more details on the latest marriage of Liz Taylor then they have on their own. Even Princess Diana's death is still discussed, and Elvis seems to be alive again for the umpteenth time. It is a tough life for celebrities because they have no privacy. I believe that their emotional breakdowns are sometimes caused not by drugs or accidents but by their fans or reporters hounding them 24 hours a day. It is sad when the hunger for more—more news, more excitement—is combined with our fear of taking risks ourselves and our belief that things come easily to well-to-do friends or celebrities.

Talk is cheap, but success must be earned. Few people see the sacrifices people must make in their lives in order to achieve and to fulfill their dreams. As a traveling businesswoman, I once heard someone describe such a life as an eternal holiday between New York, Singapore, China, and Russia. It is easy to be envious of a lifestyle that is appealing on the surface, that seems to be only exciting, smooth, and well paid. But many lifestyles might appear exotic to people who have not experienced them and are not familiar with their rigors.

I would bet that if you offered the same lifestyles to the nosy critics, including the burdens of success such as loneliness, hard work, stress, and decision-making, they would not want to accept them. They are busy talking and merely observing. They love to be spectators. It that were not so, they would be busy working on their own lives.

The truth is that we are basically made up of the same elements when we are born. The truth is that despite a hard childhood or a poor or mediocre background, we can build something with our lives and realize our dreams. Dedication and hard work as well as patience and trust are required. Persistence and the capacity to stand back up after each fall are also necessary.

Stop talking and start building your own life. If you do so, you will have no time left to concentrate on the tragic love story of a distant royal family member and you will start to feel compassion for your friends instead of envy and competitiveness.

By the time I finish with my makeup before going to Tommie's company Christmas party, I decide that this time, when my social friends start such topics, I am just going to turn away and join another group. Or maybe I will tell them that, indeed, Gary is deserving of his new girlfriend. In fact, they deserve each other! You know why? Because they went out and they searched for what they wanted. Being aware is the first step. Being engaged in endless, exuberant discussions won't change that truth. But actually, I have grown tired of all of those meaningless conversations, and I have decided just to let go of them.

December 28, 1999

➢ You Are Not Perfect: So What?

My God, it is already 5:30 a.m. Quickly, we get up and make breakfast. We rush to the bathroom just to get a quick shower and to get into some clothing. It is a bright new day, but we didn't take the time to be grateful or to discover that winter is over and the first birds are singing in the spring sky. Rushing to the kitchen, we are teetering between worrying over a newly discovered wrinkle on our face and the horror of piles of documents and full calendars awaiting us at work. We worry because we believe everything has to be done perfectly. We have a concept of perfection in our minds—started in childhood and developed over the years—that says everything must be perfect for us to function and be happy.

The house must be perfectly clean and all work must be perfectly done before we can sit down and relax or take some time off for ourselves. Many people actually do not rest until they die. They do not believe they are entitled to take time to do things that matter most to them. Sad! My choice is to complete the important things, the things that have to be completed, and to reserve the rest of my energy for things I enjoy doing on my own or with people who are fun to be with.

➢ The Great Value of Little Things

India and its wonderful people taught me to have respect for the little things in life. I learned to cherish small blessings that are hardly acknowledged in the Western world, blessings like having enough food to eat and clean water to drink, having a shower and shelter.

Many of the people in India live in the streets; they do not think about tomorrow. They fight the battle to survive only today. Many of them wish to leave and move to the West. They do not know that they would do so only to encounter a poverty that goes beyond empty stomachs and unworthy living conditions. The lack of caring and love and the greed for power and money would hit them in their hearts.

Part 3

<u>THE BRIGHTNESS OF THE STARS</u>

"Let the brilliance of the glowing stars
remind you of that golden treasure,
that beauty within you.
No one can take it away from you.
Like the stars in the night
it will shine all through your life
once you have the courage to look inside
and choose to reveal your treasure."   (D.S.)

There is light at the end of the night. It is the stars shining and preparing us for the immense warmth and illumination that await us at the dawning of each new morning. The multitude of stars reminds us that light is everywhere during our journey.

When we believe that the darkness out there will never end and that no one cares for us in our loneliness, the beauty of the stars in the dark night manifests the idea that darkness alone does not exist and that we encounter light and joy even in the darkest of moments. We need to open our eyes—the windows to our soul—and allow the light to enter. It will give us the strength to walk our road without taking a shortcut, to walk step by step on the path that leads us to that golden shrine, the treasure within.

Along the way we have to accept many facts of life that we cannot change. However, we can choose our attitudes and reactions to whatever happens. We need to know in our hearts that in order to have a harmonious and content life, it is necessary to accept life's challenges. Even if we choose to run away, we cannot find a secure hiding place for long.

We can never succeed unless we master and overcome the tough times. Our lessons will be repeated until we have undergone the necessary growth and accepted the change for the better.

➢ Immediately Please

Immediate, cheap (even better, free), and top quality: These are the requirements for the purchase of any product in the Singapore stone and construction industry.

The order won't be placed until the last minute. The bargaining never ends, not even after the purchase order is signed. Cheaper, cheaper, consistent quality—only the best. And regarding delivery, it should have been installed yesterday, so you need to deliver it as soon as possible. But "as soon as possible" for regular shipment time from Italy runs up to 21 days. Help, please, I need a magician. Maybe if I close my eyes and I pray hard enough ... No, not possible!

It is a game that we all know well: the client, the supplier, and the agent (me). Some nights I would wake up sweating from a dream in which another angry client insists on my making the impossible possible: the immediate delivery of 10,000 square meters of specially cut and polished black granite, now. He threatens me, criticizing my price. The competition has, in the client's own words, dropped the price to zero. Actually, they would pay him now, says my client, to take material from them. They would pay *him* to give *them* orders. The competition would work for free while I am asking for money and cannot even deliver today!

I awaken and look at the clock next to my bed. It is three o'clock in the morning. Relieved, I turn around and see Tommie sleeping next to me. My heart still beats fast when I realize that I am out of that never-ending circle of power mongering, beyond the reach of the pressure to get everything immediately and gratuitously. I am glad I have made up my mind. I am glad I have chosen to let go of that life.

I am able to view the eight years I spent living that life from a distance. I remember my grandmother saying: "There is no such thing as cheap and good, and never let anyone tell you differently. To produce a good product or to work for a good thing, you need time. Don't ever let anyone rush you." Thinking back on my years in the stone industry, I must admit that I always felt like a rabbit trying to escape its hunter even at the same time I was keeping the enemy satisfied during the chase.

I learned to be more productive than during those days, when seven days a week were not enough to satisfy the never-ending demands of my clients and to take part in the endless discussions with my suppliers, when weeks and months passed before any commission payments could be collected.

More is not always better, and speed does not necessarily produce the best outcome. From a distance, I have observed that my customers and suppliers, as well as those of many other industries, handle their business and responsibilities using emergency management. Battling with ever-new urgencies on the job, we allow the theory of short-term planning to rule our private lives. We do not have to! Emergencies should never run our lives. Almost everything can wait and is not necessary immediately.

➢ Individuality

I was bought up to believe that we are what other people think of us. Ironically, the more jealous other people were, the more loudly they would talk about us. In spite of their talk, our lives would get better, and in turn, we would be happier with our own lives. I have never quite understood the concept of perceiving ourselves through other people's eyes.

However, I did my best to be comfortable in situations involving controversy. On one hand, I tried to obtain the respect and acceptance of the group, and on the other hand, I tried through overachievement and steady competition to be the fastest runner and the most intelligent person in school.

Only over time did I learn that no one else, apart from ourselves, determines what we are worth and whether or not we succeed in our lives. We do not need to excel to get the attention of others, nor do we have to be "yes women" to fit perfectly into society.

What we need is to discover our individuality and to trust ourselves. We do not have to live up to anyone's values and standards except our own. Sometimes we need to forget about winning, about being faster and better, and we have to surrender and listen. True friends do not judge us according to superficial values, nor do they admire us for always being the best. They cherish us because we care and show compassion, because we understand and also need to be understood. Often we lose sight of the fact that life is very simple.

➢ Hoping and Guessing

We have been hoping and guessing for eight weeks now, weeks that seem like months or even years. I am impatient by nature, and I am working on calming my temperament, as I am told it is a negative trait.

Sometimes I wonder if it would be easier for me if I would manage life in a more relaxed way. Things meant to be always will happen, the adage says. Let it go. Just lean back and relax.

This is easier said than done. Let go and let God take control. Yes, I believe in God. I want to trust and I do trust, but still how do I let go? How can I be content enough to let go? I wonder, even though I know I have done all I can.

Sometimes I wish I could be like my friends, Siew Ling

or Tom. They can relax once they have given their best, just relax and wait for the outcome. I still stumble sometimes and fall back into old behavior patterns.

Here we are, awaiting news for eight weeks in regard to Tom's transfer. Eight weeks in a lifetime seems like so little, but eight weeks in a place you would like to leave can feel like forever.

Actually it is not bad. We have a nice apartment, more than just a roof over our heads. We have sufficient food to eat, more than merely a meal a day. And we have each other, every day.

Something urges me from inside, that little voice within me, the one I heard the first time when I was five. It says, "You need to discover new places, you need more, and you are not allowed to sit still even for a short period! You need to move, you need to be free, and you need to make money!"

I listen quietly this time. I just listen, without movement. The little voice comes and screams inside me and tries to provoke an immediate reply. But I am just listening. The voice gets louder and louder. Suddenly it disappears, tired of waiting for an answer. We need so many things, but do we *really* need them, and whoever told us that we do? Is it old patterns learned from our parents and friends, or just us?

Life does not have to be complicated. It can be simple. I learn this each day: simple food, simple answers, simple clothing, simple decisions one at a time.

In the beginning, I was afraid. I thought I could not survive staying here for one more month, and I was worried. Now Tom's transfer is approved. Instead of being happy, I am discontent because I do not have the exact date and place of the relocation. I also want to organize my life, I claim.

I say that once we have the date, I should be happy and accept it, but I am afraid that I will get worried and upset again about going to the new place. It might not be exactly what I wanted or expected. The little voice may come back and sneak into my mind again—if I choose to let it in. I am in agony! Things could be better. They always can. We forget, however, that they always can be worse too.

If you cannot make things better, do not make them worse. Work toward your dream, and you are on the way. Accept every day's challenges as lessons you need to learn on the way to reaching your dreams. The faster we learn to accept ourselves and that life is not perfect, the closer we are to our dreams and goals.

We can decide to be the best player on our one-man team on the way to winning the biggest reward ever: Life's World Cup. And remember, we are playing alone on our team because we alone are responsible for our decisions. Let's take the time to make the right ones. Let's not rush. Time is all we have: This is the time of our lives.

Let's be patient with ourselves. Remember: One says even to build Rome, more than one day was needed, and that was with the energies of thousands of people.

December 23, 1999

✎ You might be interested to know that we are moving in December 2000. I am no longer impatient. I am looking forward to our international transfer. The past months taught me to have faith and that, if we are happy with ourselves, we can even stay in a place that we do not rate in our Top 10.

May 2000

➤ To a Good Friend

I am blessed. Despite daily problems and self-created hardships, I have a few good friends. My life in Singapore as an independent businesswoman taught me many lessons. I never passed my tests the first time. I had to repeat them over and over again. Some lessons I am still learning. I am talking about the lessons of trusting and letting go.

During the last months before I left Singapore, I was under extreme financial pressure. My business was moving, but I depended on commission payments from abroad to make my way.

I had started my own business without having any capital, resources, or dependable income. I had not planned ahead financially during my full-time employment as an international marketing manager. Furthermore, I had been a big-time spender with lonely woman syndrome, wasting money on clothing, outings, and expensive holidays but never being able to relax. I have not lost my interest in shopping, but I had to learn the hard way that buying one dress instead of seven can be more gratifying.

Fine dinners can be brilliant occasions, but they should be held in the company of caring friends. Holidays are for relaxation, not for temporarily running away from our fears. Whatever we have done, it is done. The past is long gone, and the future is not yet ours.

Instead, we should live in the present and straighten out one thing at a time. There might still be things in the past that we have to take care of; confronting them helps us to solve them one day at a time. The most important thing is to learn and to create new, healthier life patterns.

During those troubled times when we tried to find ourselves, sometimes we had friends around who helped us. They knew that we needed them in those moments. Those few friends knew us very well.

I remember a friend telling me that, in times of distress, we must not run away but stand still, reflect, and admit the truth. It takes courage to admit to ourselves that we are actually in trouble, that we have to change our lifestyle and our attitudes. Sometimes we have to adjust our expectations and be patient. We must accept that things often end up differently from what we originally expected.

People who stand by us in moments of despair and who have the concern and courage to tell us their frank opinions when we are in denial are true friends. Friends who wish us well and want to see us happy and content are precious. I have promised myself to keep them around, and it is important for me that they know how much they are appreciated in my life. My metaphor for friendship is a two-way highway on which friends meet in the middle.

December 26, 1999

➢ Between Yesterday and Tomorrow

This was a first for me: the first time back to the university, back to school, not that I wouldn't have attended school eventually. Life, the eternal teacher, has molded and changed me continuously since I was 18. To survive and to be happy and content in life, I had to learn to alter my attitudes. My professors won't be able to teach me as much wisdom as life herself has, but they can pass on knowledge and they can share their experiences.

I look around the classroom and lecture halls. I see many young and beautiful people with bright futures waiting to be discovered. How many will succeed or fail? What is the definition of success? How many will be content and self-accepting, compassionate, and willing to give love and understanding back to their loved ones and to society?

It is refreshing to see so many young faces preparing for life. Many do not know yet that the biggest lessons are never taught in school. Do they know that even the professor surrenders to the fact that in the test of life he could never score 100 percent? Or that sometimes we score 100 percent, and we are still not happy? Are they aware that life is not a multiple-choice test, not a guessing game?

No answer is 100 percent right or wrong in life. The answers are called decisions, and they determine our plan of study, our road map for the school of life.

Looking into the faces of my younger fellow students makes me smile in silence: so many dreams, so many roads to choose among. It was often scary and confusing for me when I was their age. Do they feel the same way? I search in the depths of their eyes for reflections of their souls. In some, I can already see the serenity of compassion and love. In many others, I just see the expression of "Let's get this lesson over with. Let me go back to living my life." What did life mean to me then? Music, dancing, studying, traveling?

Many of my fellow students study to please society or their families, or they are only thinking about making money and moving out on their own. They have a long way to go to identify the road they want to travel, and I recognize that it is perfectly all right: They have time to discover it all. The divine pattern is working in their lives.

For me, time is much more precious today than it was in my early high school and university years. Thinking back to those days makes me smile with relief. Today I am much more focused, and I see a definite purpose in life. So I can feel the waves of excitement about life flowing out of these unique young students. I am happy that I have passed through this phase of life. As exciting as it was, today I remember its restlessness and the "importance" of many very insignificant details.

Because I am more settled emotionally, I can focus my energy on my courses and studies today. I am happier with myself because I have learned that professional success does not bring satisfaction if you're not in a field you are really committed to. The same is true of partnerships and friendships.

As much as I enjoy around me the atmosphere of youthful astonishment about life, and as much as I breathe in the fresh breeze of hope, I can't stop thinking about how much different it was for me when I was a young woman.

The loud music blaring from one of the cars driving by interrupts my thoughts. Class is over. Well, I guess I'm older but much happier, more content. Even if I could, I would not want to go back. All phases of experience are part of the human life span: We have to complete them, and they complement each other. I think, "Wouldn't it be terrible if I had not changed my attitudes and ways of thinking, my reactions and my ways of interacting with people?" It would be terrible if no change had taken place.

I feel compassion and understanding—joy in my heart—for these young people on campus. They need their own time to discover life and to find themselves. Painful lessons and happy days are still waiting for them to experience. If only I had known then what I know now. But I didn't, and it was also okay for me, just as it is all right for them.

➤ The Chat

Let's start by saying that men chat at least as much as women, if not more. Their discussions might be less intimate than women's, but the amount of talking is the same.

There is always a lot of discussion going on everywhere around us. We try to hold a conversation while listening to the news or to some music, or while watching a movie. We seldom focus on what we are doing; seldom do we give others our full attention. We overestimate our capability as sentient beings by trying to use our five senses all at one time.

We talk more but convey less meaning. We love talk shows. They are often staged or they shift facts around. They are based on gossip.

Our conversations at work, at home, and with friends are getting more superficial even as the use of sophisticated words increases. The sad thing is that if everyone is talking, no ears are left to listen. While I am standing in line at the supermarket, I see a headline: "Secret woman in Kennedy Jr.'s life discovered after his death." The liberty to write includes that anyone can write anything. What about boundaries? Boundaries and limits are not respected even after people's deaths. Privacy does not exist.

When will it ever end? Why can't we communicate in a positive way and talk about positive events? Do we always need scandals? Life is a gift, and it's full of beauty.

How is it possible that private matters appear as newspaper headlines and in daily conversations? We are lucky to know that there are friends with whom we can just sit and enjoy a quiet moment when we are afraid to be bothered with the latest affairs of the world.

➢ Soulmates

Most of the people I have met are living in different environments than I live in and have very individual views. This can lead to serious misunderstandings and communication problems when we need to share an opinion or work together for long periods. Differences can jeopardize relationships when we are not aware that our partner or friend might have different expectations and perceptions in his or her own inner world.

We have to tone down our insistence, to adjust to circumstances, and to meet others in the middle if we want to come together and stay together, if we want to avoid constant pain and nerve-wracking fights. It seems, therefore, like a miracle when we meet a friend or a complete stranger with whom we can connect deeply. We feel we are understood beyond words. We feel that we can connect and look into the soul of the other person. We can share laughter, and for the people around us, our bond is hard to understand. We need to cherish that special person with whom we are able to live in the same interior world. It is beautiful to experience these connections and to feel them grow into friendships that are long-term, that are for life.

My special friend, Siew Ling, and I are in the same interior world. We share a secret pact, an understanding like no other, and it makes us soulmates. Who knows, perhaps we were together even in our past lives?

Over the years, we learn to deal with difficult people, especially with people who are different from ourselves, each in her own complex, interior world. We learn to adjust, to compromise, and to accept each other in our separateness. Over time, we can appreciate a soulmate, someone who understands without words, who shares unspoken thoughts. Of the various gifts life bestows, this is one of the greatest.

➣ **Keep the Thought**

How sad the Third World is. This topic arises during a lecture. The Third World is a real picture in my mind, a picture that is more concrete for me than it is in the minds of most of the students. In these moments, I miss Asia very much, especially India. Nothing compares to the place you have chosen to be your home. We do not appreciate people second guessing our homes and judging our values, systems, structures, and people they do not know and will never understand by sitting in a classroom miles and miles away.

I hear that mothers in the Third World might love their children less because they have so many children and they expect that some will die of diseases. I want to scream: "Have you ever seen the pain in the eyes of a woman whose child is dying?" It does not matter how many children you have. It does not mean less to you when you lose a loved one. For now, however, I keep my thoughts to myself. I get calm and quiet, and I find peace in my soul. I would not expect them to understand, not now, during a discussion such as this.

I tried for years to understand the cycle of the world, the differences in lifestyles and culture. I concluded that the mystery of life remains unsolved, but I continue to learn. I am learning now about America.

My heart starts beating faster, and I have to consciously stop myself from interfering in the discussion. I follow for a while, but my thoughts move away to that India I know and learned to love, to its friendly people, to its hardworking middle class, and to its poorest of the poor.

I see pictures of beautiful women in colorful saris walking along muddy streets. They are smiling and chatting while they wait for an overcrowded bus. The less fortunate ones are still carrying heavy baskets filled with rocks and sand on their heads. For the meager pay of a few rupees, they are offering their energy and strength to a well-to-do construction company that is building a new five-star hotel. They will never be allowed to enter the hotel once the construction is finished. They will never cross the beautiful interiors and see the designs of the hotel lobby.

Sometimes it is not necessary to share all of our knowledge or to insist on the importance of our point during every discussion. Sometimes we are aggressively promoting our point of view, and we might even be right. A person who has experienced the facts can silently understand, while an individual who has never experienced the same things cannot believe certain realities. I learned to keep memories and facts inside my heart. It helps me to smile and to let go.

February 2000

➤ Agree to Disagree

Life becomes easier once we realize that we do not have to agree with everything or everyone. Opinions and decisions are as individual as the people who make them. People are free to decide and to choose what they want in their lives. We can make up our minds and reach out for what we desire in our private lives as well as in our careers. We do not have to please people; we do not need them to back up our decisions all the time or even at all. As long as we are happy with our choices and realize that we are the ones to live with them, our minds are free and our hearts are at ease.

When we accept that disagreement will always be a part of our lives, we can let go and accept the fact that we can agree to disagree. Trusting in ourselves and in our decisions brings us further along on the way to happiness and tranquility. Making decisions and acting on them takes us forward on our way to the hidden treasure, our soul. We learn that we do not have to be envious of other people's lives since we are in charge of our choices in our own lives. We can stand up for our choices. Let us learn to agree to disagree with people's behaviors, their attitudes, and their decisions. If a situation does not deserve our energy, then let it go. If we have the need to voice our disagreement, let us do it gently and with respect. We must respect that each of us is unique.

➤ For Better or Worse

Growing up, we were told to make secure and calculable choices. We girls especially have been told to be "safe instead of sorry." It is better to be less aggressive and more feminine: Someone might fear you are competitive. Choose the right direction in school and a vocation suitable for a woman, and go for a safe job, preferably in an office. Even if you are a good student, being a secretary is okay. If you have the firm intention to study, then become a teacher, a good job for women.

Make the right choice by finding Mr. Right. The right man will take care of you because you are not complete on your own. To be a full person, we are told, we need a counterpart who can provide and care for us, a counterpart who is in charge. Wait for the right person to come along. Much later, we are long since grown up, but we are still looking for Mr. Right.

One morning we wake up and think about the women who taught us all the things that complicate our lives, all the hurts that diminish us as women, old beliefs that hold us back from being a woman with or without a partner. We look back and analyze the relationships of our mothers. We might think of Aunt Jackie in Australia. We realize that those women do not know anything about the life of a single, ambitious businesswoman as we do.

The modern woman demands more than financial security, honesty, love, and understanding from Mr. Right. Today, a functional relationship is made up of two independent people who have decided to share their lives. Each individual is in charge and responsible for the relationship. The constant exchange of thoughts and the trust we build are important. Our choice of a life partner has been conditioned by ideas that were planted in our minds and modeled by our mothers in early childhood. Looking back and evaluating objectively the rules of how to choose, how to behave, and what a woman needs cannot be valid for us even though they might have been valid for Mom's generation.

Our lives are more complex today, and we must base our choices on the fact that we are complete even without a male counterpart. If a partnership takes more than it gives and hurts more than it complements and enriches our lives, then we must let go of it. More and more women realize that harmony lies first in themselves, and they choose a rewarding partnership that gives as much as it takes.

➤ Those Who Have It All

By the age of 48, Veenu had been divorced for 10 years. While her eldest daughter was married and living in Delhi, her sons completed their studies in the United States. Veenu had lived in the United States herself more than 20 years previously. She was there with her husband, who completed his studies in the United States, and she had lived in Washington for a year. Even during that time, she spent long hours recollecting her early childhood. She was born in northern India as the youngest child of an early Indian industrialist. She was brought up in luxury on one of India's biggest tea plantations, which was owned by her father. She ate from golden plates, surrounded by servants, and worries were kept distant from her.

Even after her divorce, Veenu has not lacked material wealth. In the 10 years following her divorce, she became more independent. She also started to smoke and to drink once in a while. She remained in their beautiful house in Madras even though her husband left for America with his new wife.

All that Veenu knows is that the last 10 years have been very lonely. They have also been a growing experience. All the while, she was missing the love and happiness only a companion could give. Occasionally, she went out with her friends or gave a party herself, but she did not ever meet a person who was available for a relationship.

Veenu was still an attractive woman, and admirers were numerous, but she was not attracted to most of them. She knew that as a divorced, wealthy woman in India, she had to be attentive to her situation. She would never make a fool out of herself. She did not give in to one-night stands, and she did not fall for married men looking for affairs.

Then she met Shiva, who was introduced to her by an old friend in the bar of her favorite hotel. He had left India and settled in Malaysia many years before. He had made a fortune in business and was in town for work. The moment they met, they fell in love. They started to see each other, and both were ready for a relationship. Shiva had to leave Madras very soon after they met because his business obligations called him home to Kuala Lumpur. He continued to call Veenu several times a day, and he returned after two weeks.

While they were spending a weekend on the beach of Goa, he told her for the first time that he wanted to marry her. Veenu thought it was too soon. However, she knew she had found love and emotional security after waiting for a long period of time. They agreed to meet in London after two weeks and to have a fabulous time. They also decided that Shiva would live in Veenu's house during his future visits to Madras.

Veenu and Shiva are still together. Everything is perfect even though they can only spend two weeks together each month. Shiva, you see, is married back in Malaysia, and he has two small children. Veenu met his wife, who does not know about their relationship. Veenu tells me today that she does not want to break up a family, that her relationship with Shiva is rewarding for her. He calls every day, and she says that they are just like an ordinary couple when he is in town and when they are overseas.

Veenu's adult children know about her relationship with Shiva—and they approve of it. Veenu has been particularly happy. Her eldest son finished his studies in New York and plans to return to Madras. Her house will be livelier again.

Veenu has mentioned to me that she wants stability. She wants to approach Shiva and ask him about marriage. Because he lives in Malaysia, she does not know if he has converted to Islam. In this case, a second marriage—in addition to Shiva's existing marriage—would be possible and approved by the state of Malaysia.

Veenu desires an official place in life at the side of Shiva, which is very important for her standing in society. She says that she needs time to herself and that being with Shiva 10 days a month is rewarding enough. She goes on to tell me that every time she is with Shiva, she is so absorbed in his presence that she forgets to ask him about marriage. He might not be Muslim, and polygamy would then be out of the question. What then?

I ask myself how it must feel to be torn between loneliness and having a relationship with clarity. I don't yet understand what there is to lose. My friend is a beautiful and wealthy woman. She dedicates time to charitable activities, and she has founded schools for women's education in India. She is a lovely person who can fulfill her every dream, except for that of a totally committed partnership. I am not sure if a part-time commitment is truly satisfying for her. I keep telling her to continue looking for an available partner. She understands, but her heart remains committed to a part-time lover.

Part 4

<u>THE WARMTH OF THE SUN</u>

"Treasure that special moment early in the day
when the sun rises. With her rays she transforms
every night into a splendid, new morning.
Absorb the beauty of the divine pattern of the rising
and setting sun day by day and find comfort
knowing that the darkness in our lives will end
when we are ready to discover the brightness
and beauty of life. In the midday let the rays of the sun
warm your soul and gently caress your skin.
Feel that heavenly warmth prevail always.
Cherish these late afternoons and serene evenings
when the miracle called sunset
turns the intense color of gold slowly into
orange and red. As the sun sets in harmony,
put your mind at ease and let your thoughts
flow freely. Inner peace appears when
you trust that the eternal sun will return
tomorrow with a new day and a new
opportunity." (D.S.)

Reaching the peak of life's mountain is not an easy journey. It will never end as long as we live. On our long way home, many times we feared failure: We feared not making it, but here we are. We can manage more than we ever imagined. We are so much more than we ever knew and dreamt about. We are more appreciated and loved since we are more loving toward others and ourselves. We are more trustworthy because we listen to our own inner voice and we respect ourselves. We are now able to enjoy the silence of a moment and the warmth of the sun shining straight into our souls. Light and sun are metaphors for love and a nurtured soul, while darkness is tantamount to fear and abandonment.

The times we thought we felt lonely as we wandered on the path of life all make sense to us now. Let us celebrate the newly discovered depth and warmth of life, the brilliance of the moment, and the perfect harmony we find inside ourselves.

➤ The Greatest Gifts of All: Time and Compassion

Time is very precious because when it is gone it will never come back. A busy person who has learned to set her own pace and her own path has discovered that time is more precious than money. It brings immense joy when wisely spent in proper doses or shared with the people we care for and where we can make a difference. It multiplies faster than money invested in the bank, and its return is higher than that of interest received from any financial institution.

Time and compassion are the greatest gifts of all. Spend

time with your loved ones because you never know when it will be their time to go. Do it for them, but be aware that your days also are already counted.

No money can buy the time and experiences shared with a parent or child, especially with your elderly parents, friends, and relatives. Let us spend time with them. Let them feel that they are important in our lives. We can make a difference. A word to a lonely stranger can mean more than winning the jackpot in the lottery. We all need love, we all need affection, and we all have fears, hopes, and dreams. Let us share them.

Close your eyes for a moment. Imagine yourself back in touch with your childhood dreams and expectations. Look at your situation right now. Spend some time with yourself. Start to accept yourself unconditionally.

True courage lies in the heart. We need to use it to discover ourselves and to reestablish our values and the priorities we give to things.

➢ New York

I remember the first time I laid my eyes on that beautiful city. Actually, my eyes were focused on a poster that my grandmother had bought for me in Germany. I was about nine years old. It was of a New York City sunset, black and dark red between the highest buildings that I could have ever envisioned.

I hung it on the wall next to my bed, and every night before I went to sleep, I showed my Grandma that special floor in the tallest of the buildings. I told her that it would be my office one day. I was very particular about the floor and windows I picked. It would be the entire floor. Every morning when I got up, I took a close look at my city, my future home, and my dream sprouted wings. Taking flight, I became a citizen of New York.

If you can dream it, you can begin it. Ultimately you will do it. Now at 29, I have traveled a great deal and I have seen the world. It is Christmas 1999, and I am in the United States. I am in Texas, but my childhood dream is alive. I am leaving for New York—soon, very soon.

By February, my time will come. I have seen the most beautiful places in the world but what does it mean? Finally I will be visiting the one city I have loved all my life. I wonder if Herbert Pfeifer's statement about New York is true: "No place on earth unveils more contrast"? I have experienced enough cities to compare it to, or maybe not. I have traveled all over, but no other place could live up to my dream, New York City. Lately I am getting mellower. I am mellower with cities and with people, with friends and with strangers. I am aware that if everything and every person would live up to the high expectation of my dreams, life would no longer be challenging.

I find time to remind myself that external beauty and short-term excitement are not worth inner turmoil and loneliness. We live in beautiful cities, have exciting friends, and are well-known guests at exclusive restaurants and bars, but our souls and our hearts often remain lonely.

December 24, 1999

➢ Home in the Garden City

How beautiful Singapore appears once you step out of the airport. I love the moment when the first hot, humid air strikes my body. I am nourished by the heat and the humidity that make all foreigners sweat the very first time they step out of the cool, air-conditioned environment.

The Garden City appears like a fairy tale country painted in rich, beautiful colors with tropical plants and beautifully maintained lawns and parks. Everything seems in harmony and organized perfectly. It is a country of oriental wealth, where dreams come true.

The air is full of tropical flavors, and I spy the greenest grass I have ever seen in my life. The reds, pinks, and oranges are brilliant, and the palm trees sway under the tropical sun.

Singapore, a small spot on the world's map, is a powerful, modern state in the Asian tradition. It offers a bridge that connects the modern with the ancient. The multi-ethnic society offers exposure to different customs, of breathing in different aromas, and of learning about Asian traditions. The sound of at least four different languages and dialects is constantly in the air, including Mandarin and its various local dialects, Malay, and Tamil mixed with English.

Singapore offers shopping excitement, unbelievable beauty, and tranquility on nearby islands. The beauty of the botanical gardens can be found just a step away from a pleasant chat with a good friend over fried rice in an open-air cafe or in one of the city's five-star hotels. Here, you can have it all. For me, Singapore is a modern dream come true even as its past is still alive. While visiting Little India and Arab Street, you can experience East Asian traditions.

In Chinatown, you will find more dialects than anywhere else.

Singapore will always be my home of choice. This beautiful place taught me some of the hardest lessons in life. It helped me to discover myself, to find the meaning of life for me. I had to leave Singapore in order to understand that it is my chosen home. I had to change in order to return.

And so I *will* return, everything about my life and myself changed. With a new profession and a fulfilled partnership, I have a content soul. My best friend, Siew Ling, is still in Singapore waiting for me to come back. I can't wait to see her sparkling dark eyes again, her beautiful smile.

Singapore was hard on me because survival was challenging and the cost of living was high. I did not realize then that the problem was not Singapore, that it was me being hard on myself, spending excessively, and feeling unhappy in the most beautiful of places. Today, I have found myself and I could live in any place, at least for a certain period of time. I am no longer restless. I have made peace with myself, but my heart and soul bring me back to the city of my dreams.

Contemplating going back to Singapore for good, I smile while I picture myself preparing our suitcases. I have learned that very little is necessary in order to be content. One suitcase is enough. It will take several months before we return for good, but time does not matter now because I understand that we will ultimately go where our hearts lead us. For me it is Asia; it is Singapore.

➤ On Punctuality and Other Promises

Promises, we make them and we break them. Often we make them halfheartedly then don't follow through with them.

I go over that process now. I sit first and think. We all are empowered by the strength of our will: the will to keep a promise, to succeed. We are responsible for first honoring our word to ourselves.

I remember promises I made to myself, maybe in the presence of one of my best friends, just for them to be broken in the next hour. I did not want to phone a person again who had hurt me, yet I did call. It was difficult to walk my talk.

By breaking our promises without good reasons, we are hurting ourselves. Our honor suffers, and our trust in ourselves diminishes. Our willpower will decrease and our vices and weaknesses will run our lives. Our moods, not ourselves, will be in control of our lives.

How often do we say we want to lose some weight or exercise, but how long do we honor our promises and New Year's resolutions? Who are we kidding or betraying? Only ourselves. We should mean enough to ourselves; we should honor ourselves enough to break out of old, nasty patterns and embrace new ones. It is a difficult road, but we can possess our own power. No one can take it away from us if we do not allow them to or silently agree to it. Let's take a stand today. Let us look inside ourselves. Do we need to make and keep a promise to ourselves that we keep breaking? Why?

Do you know that you are the *number one* priority in your life? Do you know that you need to honor and love yourself before others will honor and love you? Keep your promises always, and you will see how consistency can build self-respect and self-worth. Learn to trust yourself and to feel compassion for your own soul. Then you will learn to respect the weaknesses of others and you can choose to deal with them or to walk away.

It is important to learn to make choices, take calculable risks, and trust ourselves. Learning to be responsible for our actions and their consequences and learning consistency in behavior are fundamental for happiness in our lives and in our relationships.

Strangely, I got all these thoughts while I was reading the notice at the administration office of our condominium: "BACK At 1:00 p.m." I had already been waiting for 20 minutes. In the old days, I would have been angry and upset: These people, telling me one thing and doing something different.

Today I am mellower and less judgmental, and I remember how often I made my friend Julaila wait more than 20 minutes for me. I made her wait to get together for a cup of coffee in town, for dinners, and for lunches. I told her I was sorry, but I did not try on our next date to make it on time.

Today I honor my promises, be they over business meetings or coffee appointments. I try hard to make it on time. If I cannot make it, I will give a call and advise the other person of the situation. This is also called respect, tolerance, friendship, and professionalism.

"… after all those tears," Simply Red sings over the radio. After 25 years, Tim and Laura finally got divorced. They were living under one roof for 25 years, but for the last 17, they had been more companions than husband and wife. They had lived in a ferocious, hate-love relationship for half their lives. Laura had become an alcoholic and Tim a workaholic with severe heart problems. The marriage was not helping either of them. Laura blamed her husband, who was always away for business, for her alcoholism, and Tim resented her but still loved her. He was also afraid that she would go downhill once he left her. Laura had been in and out of hospitals and was getting constant therapeutic treatment.

After their separation, Laura went to the hospital again, and their fight over money went on for months. They are no longer in touch now. Both have started new lives.

Tim told me he knew after the divorce that everything would fall into place. It took him 25 years to become emotionally independent. He had been codependent with his alcoholic wife.

Laura, on the other hand, stopped blaming her drinking problem only on her ex-husband. After being sober for eight months, she began the process of growing up. She had married at the age of 17, moving away from her family and into a marriage with a far older partner. She never had time to grow or develop. She let herself be shaped by others. Tim was dominant in the relationship, at least in the first few years. Laura told me she did not know how to laugh anymore. Now she can.

Both have new friends; eventually both found new partners. Today both agree that they should have ended their marriage years earlier.

February 2000

➤ The Christmas Tree

Have you ever passed by a building that you are sure you've never seen before, but it brought back memories, good memories of freedom and peace? Or you look into a pair of eyes among strangers, and they give you comfort and hope?

I always feel comfort and hope when passing by a Christmas tree or when observing the snow falling on an evening before Christmas. The green of the tree reminds me of my peaceful childhood and the excitement of waiting for Santa to come and visit. It reminds me of beautiful voices in the church with the choir singing for the holiday and beautiful angel-like voices bringing us nearer to God. The negativity of the world seems to disappear in these moments. Harmony and love fill our hearts.

I have seen many Christmas trees this year here in Texas. The most beautiful ones were in a nearby shopping center and in the administration office of our condominium. And I have my own tree. The lights are glowing day and night, and the peaceful sigh of its green branches makes me feel at ease.

We should have Christmas trees all through the year if it would help to make people feel at ease, at home on Earth, and closer to their neighbors.

December 24, 1999

➤ As Time Goes By—The Millennium

I cannot escape the terrific excitement of the coming New Year and the last days of the departing old year. I am reminded of the "event of the century" by well-meaning calls, cards, and wishes from people in stores and during Christmas parties. Nevertheless, I like to believe that my music plays a different tune, in a different rhythm.

My music is daily life. The melodies are life's eternal changes, and the rhythm is directed by my inner clock, not by a calendar page called December that turns once a month.

Excitement and reflection mark our days before the coming of the new year, and we are aware that another year is coming to an end, 365 days, each of which was a witness of life, each of which was precious. Do we really need to turn December's calendar page to value our existence? I don't think so. Every ordinary day can be a *new year,* and a *new start* in our lives if we choose it to be. The turning of a page does not determine our success or failure, our happiness or despair, or our fulfillment or dissatisfaction. The determination lies within us. We are, at this moment, *exactly* where we choose to be. We can change today and make the true new year start the minute our decision has been made.

When we use our unlimited energy, we put our power to work. Do it now! Don't wait for a calendar page to turn for a new year to arrive. Do it now and excel. Excel in life, love, and work.

Don't give away your responsibility for changing your life to a calendar page called December. If you do not attempt to change your life yourself, nothing will be different with the start of a new January but the number of the year.

We can whistle the tune of "What's another year?" and wait our entire life until the calendar page won't turn for us anymore. Or we can make the most of that treasure called life. We can enjoy all of its shades—bright spring, shining summer, brown autumn, and snow-white winter—as challenging, ever-new seasons.

My inner clock ticks louder than the world's exterior clock today, louder than it did in my early youth when the external features of the ending year had a direct impact on my soul. Today I enjoy celebrating with a small circle of friends, away from the media and parties. I like to share the good and the not-so-happy experiences encountered during the year with a few friends. At midnight, we smile together upon a new calendar page called January. The adventure of life continues.

➤ Forgive and Forget

Forgiving is sometimes a difficult task because we are afraid to let go of familiar feelings of pain, hate, and misunderstanding; feelings of being judged unjustly; and feelings of having been wronged by others. Forgiving means accepting that a painful memory or a humiliation happened in the past, but that we live in the present. We need to make space in our hearts for new, positive feelings. Forgiving means clearing up old "bills" and writing off old "debits." We must let go of the need to pay back. Forgiving means letting go of pain and sorrow and focusing our energy on the present instead of being caught up in the past.

While my eyes are wandering over the green meadows

of Texas, I can't help recalling Clarisse, and I try to imagine how difficult it must be to forgive and forget that kind of loss: a country, a home, a family, a tribe.

I met Clarisse in Kuala Lumpur. With her serious, dark eyes and long, black hair, she had very distinct features. She was Canadian, and she had come to Malaysia from Dublin with two Italian friends. They wanted to travel the world with their backpacks. In the beginning she seemed to be an ordinary young woman in love who had chosen to work overseas in order to discover the world. In Dublin she had fallen in love with Giuliano, a young Italian.

There was something about Clarisse that I could not explain. As I came to know her better, I found that she was unlike any other woman I had ever met. Then she started to tell me about her heritage. She was a Canadian Indian, and she was brought up on a reservation close to the United States border. She was a full-blood Indian, from the nation of the Mohawks. For the first time, I heard North American Indian history from an Indian. We talked not about the horrors of the past, but of the fatality of the current situation of the Indians today.

Clarisse described living on the reservation as hopeless. She talked about money subsidies from the government, monthly checks that arrived, payment made to keep the Indians away from jobs and outside of the main population, to keep them on the reservations. Therefore, the majority of men would not work, and many of them were addicted to alcohol and drugs. Clarisse explained that the spirit of the members of her community was being killed more every day.

I asked her about leaving the reservation, about education, about hope for the future generations, and about the situations of the women in the community. Clarisse was silent for a long time before she answered. She said that education, even university education, was available to Indians in Canada. But by the time young people finished high school, they had lived only in the misery found on the reservation. Their role models were men with beaten spirits who were addicted to alcohol and drugs and who were without hope.

Some of the youngsters would manage to leave and go to college or attend a university. But that meant leaving their homes to enter a world they had never been a part of and living in an environment that made it even clearer that they are a minority. Even the Indians who graduate from college have difficulty getting jobs. Clarisse did not see hope for her people on the reservation. She did not see freedom for them in Canada.

She had been married at the age of 17, a happy marriage for a couple of months. She told me about a young husband who had gradually lost his pride and his hope. She talked about frequent beatings and alcohol abuse. She escaped at the age of 22. She ran away from the reservation, working as a waitress for a few months to make enough money for a ticket out of town. She went to Dublin, where she worked for two years before she met Giuliano, who was from Naples.

She had no contact with her community back in Canada, and Dublin gave her space to breathe. She became very attached to her young fiancé. She was desperately looking for love, acceptance, and freedom. She wanted to get married in Italy and start all over. She wanted to forget. She wanted a change.

I thought I would find some Indian cultures in Texas, but sadly, I didn't find any members of the First Nations here. My eyes are opened wide while I admire the beauty of the local sunsets. The setting sun has brought back my wish to find experiences of the traditional heritage of the land. Inheritance and tradition are necessary for a country and its people to grow spiritually.

The sun rises and sets—but the Great Spirit has left, just as Clarisse left her home. Long ago the tribes were forced to leave, forced to abandon their land, their homes, their traditions, their customs. I was told to go to Oklahoma or New Mexico to find more about Indian cultures, that in Texas I would not find what I was searching for. It fills me with sadness.

I think of Clarisse, and I know that the battle of the First Nations is not over; that only the strategies have changed. No matter what, wrong never becomes right. When we listen to our hearts, we can hear the cries of the Earth: She cries for her lost friends, and she leads them to find the trail of death.

She cries because she has remained behind and lonely. The savage, now her master, is not her friend. He has set out to destroy her, as greed has destroyed him. Man needs to possess whatever he sees. But as long as the truth is alive, memories will exist: Red Indians and their families come to life. Proud hunters and beautiful women with children talk to each other in a traditional language. They believed that giving is a virtue that benefits both the giver and the receiver. They taught the settlers the mysteries of the forest, of survival. The past cannot be changed, but we can create a new future for ourselves every moment. Let us renew ourselves, our spirits.

I know how difficult it is to ask for forgiveness, to say we are sorry, but it is even more difficult to forgive. I wish you well, Clarisse.

"The most powerful emotions in life are love and fear. While fear destroys, love is accepting and forgiving, open to differences.

As a nation filled with fear we bring grief and suffering to others. As individuals we do the same to our family, to our friends and to ourselves." (Mother Teresa)

December 21, 1999

➤ Listen to the Silence

Once we take time away from our busy schedules, time away from noisy traffic, endless conversations, and raucous music, we are surprised by the soft voices within silence.

Sitting in my favorite place, I dedicate time for silent moments every day. I let my thoughts flow freely, and I admire the beauty and peace of the moment: no hassles, no telephones ringing—only that harmonious moment and myself.

Over the years, I learned to enjoy quietness, to find peace within myself and the world. My need for quiet times prevails.

➤ Money Rules the World: What Rules Your Life?

In a society where social rank, professional standing, and the size of paychecks count more than character, it is difficult at times to stick to the basic instinct that says: "Choose values over money." Building character requires strength today more than ever. Shrewd business sharks seem to be having the times of their lives. Being ruthless is *in:* In a big way the rule is, the more the better. Consideration and acceptance of others seem to be outdated and inappropriate in today's fast lifestyle. Everybody wants everything, now, at any cost. And she who possesses the power takes it all. Money *is* power: power over people and things, but not over life. We might believe that the rich always get what they want, that they are always happy—but the truth is far from it.

The richest people I have dealt with in my private and business life have been the poorest. Bored by their possessions and terrified by loneliness, the rich constantly searched for new distractions. Others, driven by the demands of work or greed for more money, did not have any consideration for other people and had become subhuman.

Honestly, are there very many people who don't agree that being rich is better and that attempting some shortcuts along the way to becoming rich can be excused? We see people succeeding—succeeding in the outer world—but we do not participate in their inner lives and their burdens.

I have settled on my own opinions after years of reflection. I have decided that there are more important issues than money. First, I need to enjoy what I do. Yes, money is important and everybody must make it, but we as people are more important. Since I stopped running after the green notes that seem to determine our lives, I took charge of my own life. And actually, by doing what I enjoy and by doing my best, the money flows easier. Give it a try.

➤ Attitudes

By going back to school, I noticed that acceptance and tolerance are necessary in order to get along in the world. All humans are different. Some are fast, some slow. Some are smarter, some less intelligent. Yet all have the same right to existence and education.

Often it is our attitude or our feelings of pride and superiority that do not allow us to connect with others, that make us impatient and unfriendly. There are many external events that we cannot influence, but there is one thing in our lives that we can always choose. This one thing is our attitude, our reaction to the outside world. While I listen to someone who still does not know that Charles Darwin is the father of the modern theory of evolution, I remind myself to be patient. There are many questions I might not be able to answer although my neighbor might excel in them. Is it really so terrible to go through learning it all over again? No, I do not think so.

I have chosen my attitude this time. I learn to be accepting and quiet. First, I look inside myself. Things do not trouble me so easily anymore, especially if I am not in charge, if it is not up to me. We are all beautiful human beings, and everyone has something to teach us.

➢ Gratitude

During different stages of our lives, we have different interests. We live in different places and environments. Sometimes we change our friends and partners. Very few people walk with us the entire way. We know that we must go through change because without change there is no growth. Yet we are terrified about anything that changes our daily routine. Even if we hate our familiar lifestyle, it is difficult to surrender to something new, even if it's something better.

Along the way, each of us meets people who influence our lives and our way of thinking. With their insights and understandings, their advice and their friendship, they help us through the dark times. They are available for serious talks or they lend a helping hand when we are moving. They give us the feeling of being accepted.

It might be a family member (a grandma in my case, or an aunt), an elder friend, a schoolmate, or a stranger you meet on the bus who gives you the answers to your questions. You just need to open your eyes. These helpful people do come along. I call them guardian angels, selfless people who mean well and are dependable.

Unfortunately, the threads of life pull us away from one another, and each one of us follows her own road. After we walk out of the darkness into the bright sunshine, we have a tendency to forget about those loving people and trusting souls who strengthened us in times of distress.

A card, a little "thank you" that says we have not forgotten about them and their selfless friendship demonstrates concern, love, and gratitude. Let's offer them a word or a phone call to let them know we are there for them, to console them or to share their joy. Let's not forget about these simple gestures, for they enlighten our hearts and help us become better people.

I am grateful to everyone who has shared their lives with me and to everyone who made a difference in my life. Thank you, thank you, and thank you.

Part 5

<u>COLORS OF THE RAINBOW</u>

"So near and yet so unbelievably far
the colors of the rainbow.
As unbelievable as the appearance
of the rainbow is the appearance of
our hidden treasure, our Soul,
once we reveal it to the world.
Our shine in the world is incomparable
and everlasting when we reveal our true colors,
when we open the gate to our deepest self
our Soul."   (D.S.)

Finally we have crossed the valley and mastered many powerful lessons. We have stepped out of the darkness into the bright light of the sun. We can accept life and our daily reality. We have learned that it is necessary to accept today, to strive for the tomorrow of our dreams. We are getting better day by day. Having discovered the brilliant colors of life does not mean that we are living in a perfect world without feeling disappointment or pain anymore. We have discovered that we can master our lives by trusting our Higher Power and ourselves.

Our approach to life—toward dealing with challenging situations—has changed. Our attitude has changed. Now we know that we are not alone and that we do not have to fight all the time. We choose our battles, and we conserve our energy for the right causes that promote a positive life attitude.

On our journey toward the colors of the rainbow, we might want to consider helping others to see the world as it really is: a beautiful constellation of opportunities and challenges waiting to be discovered.

When we are calm and trusting, positive thoughts and feelings heal our restless minds and our souls. We have learned that no one can take away our blessings, the opportunities and changes that were made for us. We have to do the best we can, then we must let go. By letting go of fear of failure, letting go of hatred and resentment, and letting go of feelings of guilt and overwhelming responsibility, we will be faced with further lessons, but we can confront them calmly. Overcoming our fear is a daily challenge. As human beings, we sometimes will still feel overwhelmed by the demands of society.

We have learned to search out our quiet place, to rest

and to meditate for a while, and we discover afresh our energy and power. We discover our own inner clock. We learn to accept our own inner timing. We know that we can be happy, no matter what, when we are balanced and in harmony with ourselves.

Compassion has outgrown jealousy and competitiveness. We are happy to give. Life is not black and white anymore. We are ready to confront our partners lovingly and to appreciate the lessons of love: trust, joy, and harmony. Accepting the divine pattern in our lives, we know that good always prevails as long as we are ready to choose it and accept it.

➣ Country of a Thousand Rainbows

I was taught the most important lessons of acceptance in India, a country inhabited by people who are considered to be the poorest of poor. This country taught me to embrace silence and to accept the immense beauty of nature found in the eternal harmony of a sunset and the early rising of the glowing sun. Never have I seen side by side the beauty of stark browns and rich oranges, of bright green trees, and of gracious poor people. Never have I encountered a country where luxury and richness are enhanced by smiles on hungry faces, by dirt in the streets, and by humbly lovable and admirable people.

➣ Cherish the Day

Letters and postcards can call our attention to a sunny foreign country where our friends spend their holidays. I have learned to believe that postcards are well-intentioned hellos from happy friends spending a vacation on a tropical island. They are well-meant and not vicious notes to make us jealous.

Today, December 8, 1999, a letter from Alexandra reached me. Alexandra is my faithful German school companion and lifelong close friend. She is married now, in the middle of building her own house and fully occupied with her little sunshine, Helena. Alexandra and I had grown up and literally grown into life together. Despite her busy schedule and our different priorities, we have maintained our friendship over the years. Like ships on a stormy ocean, we have always been in touch via phone, fax, and mail.

Alexandra's letter brought me back to our first years in high school, both of us full of promise and hope for life. We fulfilled our dreams in different ways, and in spite of all our differences and our distance, we are as close as ever.

I have not seen her for two years, but I know that, once we are together, we will sit down with a glass of wine and start talking exactly where we left off last time. Her letter tells me about her life and her daughter, Helena, who is one year old. I have been in Germany more than once since her birth, for my usual layovers in Frankfurt. Often we said we would meet—we never made it.

It was my fault because I was sticking to eternally hectic work schedules. This has changed. In my letter, I tell her that my priorities have changed, that the moment is all we have. Unfortunately, we are seldom aware of it. Today I have decided to dedicate time to the truly important things, to treasure the love I have found and the friendship that Alexandra is offering me.

I remember our first nights out together after having passed our driving tests. Our dreams were of growing up and leaving the city to discover the world. On our first holiday together in Spain, during our last school vacation, we enjoyed our carefree youth.

The only time we had grown slightly distant was when the school term ended in 1989. Alexandra was destined for Paris, the city of her dreams. She would work for one year as an *au pair* with a Parisian family. I got ready to leave for Florence, Italy, where I was about to learn Italian in an intensive language course. Later I was to visit a fashion design school. Suddenly, everything became different for the two of us.

However, both of us were so excited about the bright future awaiting us that we forgot about the present and about the support our friendship had offered us all those years. We got short-tempered and did not see much of each other before our actual departures. Once we had started to experience the real world in person instead of in pictures, books, and films, we quickly came to know that the world could be cold, lonely, and demanding as well as embracing, friendly, and rewarding.

In facing the world, however, we did not have to sacrifice a long-term friendship that had left traces in our very hearts and souls. We returned anew to our old path of friendship, cherishing it even more. Actually, the distance ultimately brought us closer.

➤ It's Over

Sha is a very attractive, young lawyer in Kuala Lumpur. As a matter of fact, her mother is one of the more famous attorneys in town and Sha, along with her three sisters, is a lawyer in her mother's firm.

Barely 25, she is one of the youngest professionals in town, and she is busy in court every day. For over eight years, she had been in a relationship with Kishore, who works as a senior lawyer in consultation with her law firm.

For five long years, he had been asking her to marry him, but she always felt that she was too young. Their relationship was beautiful in the beginning, Sha says. Kishore was caring and spent a lot of time with her, especially on the weekends. They went for dinners or to the cinema like every young couple. Kishore was 32 then and very proud of his abundant finances. Over time, things changed. They worked together in the same office when Sha started practicing law. Kishore did not call her as often as he used to and started to hang out more and more with his friends, particularly during the weekends.

He would promise to meet her and her friends, and then he wouldn't show up. Initially he called every time to advise that he might be late. When he did not show up, Sha called him back. They played cellular phone tag. However, his phone would be switched off. No reply. The suitor could not be reached. Meanwhile, Kishore continued to ask for Sha's hand. Now 37, he is ready for marriage. Actually, he wants a son. Sha, on the other hand, keeps finding fewer and fewer reasons to agree to a marriage.

Six weeks ago, they stopped talking to each other; rather, Kishore stopped talking to Sha. She does not know why. She only knows that they have nothing in common anymore: no social life, no friends, no intimacy, no sex. It is her first relationship, and she does not want to give up on it or to abandon the hopeful fragments that still might be made intact again. She tries to talk to Kishore, without success. Her calls and messages are not returned.

Finally, the news is broken: Kishore informs Sha's sister

that he is going out with someone new. He has been seeing someone for about three weeks now, and his relationship with Sha is over.

She is angry on the phone as we talk, more angry than hurt. Why couldn't he tell her? Why? After we talk for a while and I point out all the advantages her newly gained liberty will offer her, she seems calmer, confident that her life is not over.

Now, after one month, I hear that she is enjoying her freedom. She spends time with her friends and dedicates time to herself, finding out what she wants and expects from a partner. Maybe she does not want a partner in the near future. She is free.

➢ Setting Priorities

A thousand books or more have been written about life and living. Some try to give us the right direction, the right approach to a fulfilled life—whatever they mean by that— and others find the meaning of existence in a particular religion. Few authors share with us the most important point.

To handle life and to live, we need nothing more than simplicity. Let us take the complications out of our daily activities and choose our priorities carefully.

Most of us say, "Tomorrow I will change. I will look for a new job and get a better husband," and so on. Few of us think about being a better friend to ourselves first, about getting acquainted with what is inside us or the body that carries us around day after day. Once we learn about and feel what is important to us and we find the courage to live accordingly, our lives will seem to be a gift again and our living will become joyful and easy. It is all about setting our priorities and living our roles according to our own list of priorities. We might find that we have time to be better wives because we have eliminated all unnecessary activity from our agendas that previously took up so much of our days. Or we might find that we want to be loving girl-friends but we are actually coupled with the wrong partner.

Make it simple. Identify the problem and act on it. You have problems: Who doesn't? Dwelling on problems doesn't make life better. Sort it out! Find different approaches to your problems, and one option will work.

Simplicity means eliminating everything in our lives that brings us constant pain and more trouble than well-being. It might be a relationship or a friendship that is at stake.

Let it go if doing so brings you freedom and peace in the long run. Let us make one decision at a time. And never count on a second or future life: Let us appreciate the life we have.

December 26, 1999

➢ Time Changes—We Change

Ah, December 24th! The phone rings and—I'm so happy—it's my friend from Singapore wishing me Merry Christmas. I did not recognize her voice immediately. It is 10 p.m., and the glass of port has had its effect. They say a friend is just a friend, but that is not true. There are the special ones who really do love and treasure you, who care for you, and then there are those who pretend to be caring but are actually rejoicing over all the bad things happening to you.

Questions like "Did you gain weight?" and remarks like "Now you just sit around doing nothing" are not favorites for anyone. Above all, they eliminate your choices for answers. I prefer to keep quiet—to mind my own business.

Cheerfully, I announce our return to Asia by 2001, thinking my so-called friend will be delighted. "Oh, I thought you would never come back," replies a voice that is not especially excited. "Is it Singapore or Jakarta?"

"Jakarta," I answer, thinking to myself that it is time to end the conversation. "We will let you know. How about you?" Not much of a reply, and then we maintain that we will hear from each other.

"Well, Merry Christmas to you and your friend. What was his name again?"

"Tom," I reply. "All the best."

Maybe I could have been fooled one or two years ago, thinking it was so good she called for Christmas. Now times are different—I am different. I got a call from a person that never takes the time to write back, not even a postcard. She is a person who pretends to be my friend but actually hopes to dig out some areas in my life that seem miserable so she can rejoice in them. She cannot hide her annoyance over the fact that I still have not grown fat and unattractive. I thought she would share my joy that I was finally coming back home to Singapore.

Well, I did not lose a friend on that December 24th because you cannot lose something you never had. It was a sad moment. I know I have changed, and my ideas about friends and my values have changed. I said good-bye with a light heart. I recognize the true values of the real friends I have, and I rush to wish Tom a Merry Christmas.

➣ Dedication and Choosing the Right Cause

All too often we dedicate our time and our efforts to doing things that are expected of us, things that are not close to our hearts, but we do not have the courage to admit that to ourselves, let alone to others.

Unless we understand that our true values and gifts—our talents—are distinctive and given to us to build our life around, we will not feel satisfied and happy. We might be very successful, running our own or another's business, but we will often feel empty and unfulfilled. With our special gifts, we can bring joy to ourselves and to others. Reality is not first making money and then concentrating on your talents, but rather it is using your talents and making a job out of them, all while enjoying the work. The money follows automatically.

True devotion is only possible if you very strongly like what you are doing. I was caught up for 10 years in a vicious cycle of worldwide marble and granite marketing, representing various companies and serving clients' needs. Everybody told me what a brilliant, profitable business I had, what great traveling opportunities it would offer to me. I enjoyed the travel, but did I really enjoy the business? Frankly, no, I did not. It was a rough business with tricky contracts and neither side ever content with payment or the quality of materials supplied.

I rather hated the interaction with clients and companies at certain times but still made myself believe that everything was working out fine. I believed that once involved in marble and granite, one couldn't simply leave and change jobs. The career would never let you go.

These words mouthed by business insiders are a myth.

You can cut yourself loose. What we do does not determine who we are. Not even our dream job and our unique talents determine who we are. As individuals, we are much broader in interests and richer in possibilities than we can realize through our work.

We become so involved in our work and in planning the next step of the next meeting that we forget to think about and evaluate the really important things: What are we doing with our lives? Which way are we going?

Do yourself a favor: Sit back and think about the life you want and compare it with the one you are living each day. The bigger the gap between the two, the more you need to ask yourself if a lower stress level, a different job, or a new working environment would change the situation. Be honest! We always rush and run. How long does it take us to discover that life is about living? Many women miss out on that part because schedules and responsibilities seem more important than anything. Bear in mind that no one is indispensable. Someone better or worse than you, more or less dedicated, may take over your job—but the world keeps on turning.

Nowadays, I am no longer following clients' whims. Why not decide in our younger years to dedicate our time and our career to a field in which we can excel by using our personal talents?

December 27, 1999

➢ Earth and Eden

The wise woman knows that the beautiful and the ugly do not lie far apart.

It has been an extraordinarily happy and fulfilling day because the good news was broken: Tommie and I would be transferred to an overseas assignment. The chances were most likely Sao Paulo, Brazil; Milan, Italy; or the Pacific Rim. I was dying for Southeast Asia but nevertheless would have welcomed Sao Paulo or Milan. Italy was my second home. I had not been to Milan more than once during my four-and-a-half years of living in Florence.

I had received an Erasmus scholarship at Siena University as a young student, after which I had continued to study and stay in Italy. Staying there meant finding a job and making money. During my time in Italy, I was primarily staying in Florence and Massa-Carrara. I soon learned to love the southern European flair and the creative spirit of the country that produced the most talented artists the world has ever seen.

Italy and its natural beauty still make me pause and reflect. I am always longing to go back and retrace the past—my past. I lived in that beautiful country for the first time when I was 18 years old directly after college, and I was determined, first and foremost, to go to Florence to study the language.

During my two-month stay in the summer of 1988, I met one of the most important people in my life, Mrs. Alfa Ferri Morganti. She was elegant, with the look of an English aristocrat, and she would become my second grandma, in Italian *la seconda nonna*. Even today, seldom does a week pass when we do not hear from each other. The greatest gifts of all are truly selfless love and devotion, which we can find in different types of relationships.

Back in Waco, Texas, while we were celebrating the news of the transfer, the phone rang. Tom received a phone call from his three adult kids. They shared an apartment in Toledo, and Tom thought he had set them up nicely. But things always happen differently than we plan.

Young people need their own room to discover the world. Life is too short to experience alone, but most young people do not like to believe that. This is nothing new to us, and I guess we were no different. The phone call took its own course and left Tom worried and feeling responsible. The news was nothing dramatic, but they would no longer share an apartment, for all of them wanted to go their own way. Our house, which a few minutes before had seemed to overflow with joy, was now filled with a thoughtful atmosphere. Welcome back to Earth! We were already flying in higher skies and hadn't yet thanked our creator for our blessings.

➢ Careful What You Wish For

A dear and very successful friend of mine explained to me the meaning of the saying "Be careful what you wish for, you might get it" during one of our business trips to Malaysia. Vishwanath, a workaholic with the ability to grasp things quickly, has made his way in a country like India from having a very mediocre background to being an internationally recognized owner of a stone business. He put himself through engineering school and to this day works a heavy schedule, up to 14 hours per day.

He is an often-seen guest in the West-End, the Sheraton, and the Oberoy Hotels of his hometown. This was not always so. Only 15 years ago, he would not have been allowed to enter any of those establishments.

While we are sitting on the terrace of the famous Taj Restaurant, he recalls his very first visit to the same hotel about 15 years earlier. He was a professional engineer with the choice of making very little money in India or leaving for the United States. He decided to stay in India, so he left Bombay, the place of his studies, and returned to his hometown, Bangalore. Bangalore is the Silicon Valley of India.

He left his profession and obtained training from an elderly man who taught him the craft of inspecting marble and granite blocks still in their rough state before their exportation to Europe. It was the beginning of the natural-stone boom in India, and Vishwanath had his chance early. His apprenticeship was hard and was accompanied by long hours of work, which was more astonishing because he was unpaid.

Vishwanath had set his mind on being successful in business, in making money. He decided to go through those hardships for several months, even several years, to learn the new trade. Living at his parents' house, he couldn't afford to even go out with his friends anymore. He was a hardworking, busy man, but without income.

One day an important client was in town, a German buyer who had settled in Portugal. He had started to buy and import granite blocks from India. The German client had left the office of Vishwanath's boss early in the afternoon to retreat to his hotel. The man left some important sample pieces behind, and Vishwanath attempted to deliver them to the hotel.

Vishwanath found himself on the dusty road to the hotel. When he reached the gates surrounding the lawns and gardens on the premises, the guards stopped him. He was not allowed inside the hotel, and he had to leave his delivery with them. The hotel would not allow entrance to people like him, he was told.

It was then that he set his mind on succeeding. Today, those guards are still working at the Taj. He smiles and tells me, "Well, they do not recognize me, but I recognize them. Now I feel compassion, and actually, I am grateful. You can achieve everything you dream of when you put your mind to it."

For everyone, success means something different. For many, it means money and financial freedom. For others, it means harmony with themselves and their loved ones. Whatever it means, when you put your mind to it and pour your heart into it, you can achieve it. Once you have achieved it, it is up to you to decide whether it is worth the effort or if you were just hunting down a false dream.

Today, for Vishwanath, the Taj means nothing. He identifies himself neither with the high society nor with the expensive hotel. He has grown enough emotionally and spiritually to understand that the true value of a person lies deep inside the soul. It was a pleasant evening, but I become thoughtful after Vishwanath and his wife drop me off at my own hotel, also a five–star accommodation.

Be careful what you wish for. Many of us are persistent and committed to what we desire, be it obtaining a promotion or keeping a relationship going. We might fall in love with a person who does not care for us as we do for them or who is not committed as we are. We keep on calling that person, trying to change the situation. We get what we want, start a long-term relationship, and eventually get married. It does not take long to discover that the person has not changed. He still might not be committed. Now our marriage is a mistake, and our emotional security is at stake. We might separate or divorce.

Be careful what you what you wish for, you might get it—especially when it comes to a close relationship. We need to evaluate our friendships. Is he really the person we want in our lives? We need to remember that we can have only what is available in the real world. Words can lie, but actions speak clearly. A person's behavior generally mirrors his intent. It either shows interest and respect for us or neglect. We need to be careful before we focus on something and give our energy away to it. We need to make sure that the person or the cause deserves our attention.

➢ What We Own Tells Us What?

We no longer have trouble keeping the cupboards full. Instead, we are facing problems with the closets. They have to be very spacious for the immense variety of our wardrobe: clothes for dinner and dance, for business lunches and power breakfasts, clothes that are decent or provocative, sexy, elegant, or even obscene. From the various colors of stockings and high-heeled shoes to miniskirts and sport dresses, dozens of dress codes must be respected, especially by women.

In a matter of days, no one remembers who wore what first, but today it has the status of the latest fashion. It is not important if it is uncomfortable or hot: If it is in style you'd better wear it. Otherwise, questions will be asked or, worse, looks will be exchanged on your account.

On the street or at a party, you will be judged by what you wear, seldom by who you are. Your cleavage is too revealing or not revealing enough. The color suits you wonderfully or you seem very pale. Well, maybe it's just the dress.

Who has not witnessed or even participated in that kind of party talk? Well, smart women know that less is more, that simple is more elegant. Once we realize this, it does not matter what other people say about us.

And then? Okay, let us clear the cupboards and closets of all the unnecessary, lovely pieces we used to wear because they were attractive, though uncomfortable or bought in the belief that we would some day find the occasion for wearing them. For the most part, that occasion never arrived. This "clearing out" brings space into our lives. I think about the good old cupboards, simple and organized, and I smile to myself. Every single piece that we put aside to send to a charitable organization tells a story about us, the women who bought it in a moment of anger or happiness, in a time of bitter self-doubt or loneliness.

In the end, less is more. I still love shopping—but not buying! It is not necessary to buy everything our hearts desire. Possessions bring complications and responsibilities.

I remember my earlier shopping trips. They were stressful. I made the painful decision in the shop to buy everything, then the bill came a month later, and my mood switched to reality when the credit card statement arrived. Why collect more and more things that we neither wear nor need? We buy ourselves trouble.

While I am sorting out my dresses, I remember the feelings of guilt that haunted me until all my bills were paid. Once we no longer need the approval of others, our appearance and our opinions become free and easy.

As I continue clearing my closet, the free space makes me happy. There is more space in my life now. Now it is very simple to see what I need to see and easy to find what I want to wear. It is easy to give things away once we understand that contentment and self-acceptance do not come from external sources and that they certainly don't come from other people or from material purchases.

Keep your life simple where you can. Simplicity in your cupboards is a start. It will help you day by day to focus on life's important issues. And don't be afraid if your priorities are different from your neighbors' or friends'. You do not have to live with them.

December 27, 1999

➣ Unfinished Business

Happiness is in you—not in another relationship or another person. You will not find it by changing environments, jobs, apartments, or friends. Recognize that you have everything inside yourself that you need. Set your priorities: What is important to you? Who are you really? Then you are on the right road.

Along this road, you will find a healthy environment that's best for you, the right understanding, intelligent friends, and the right place to live and to work. Give it time.

➣ Jia: Fresh Wind from China

Nine months after we moved to Waco, I made my first friend. I had returned to the university to learn about why we behave and act the way we do. I started to study psychology.

Where I was brought up, people thought that psychologists were crazy and that they needed professional help themselves. They believed that psychologists used their studies to try to overcome their own problems first, and there might be a bit of truth in these words.

I met Jia at the foreign language department of Baylor University in Waco. She was sitting at her computer, and I just had to talk to her. I found out that she was a guest professor from Tsinghua University in Beijing, China. Her specialty was English, but while in America, she taught Chinese. We started to talk about China, about Beijing. We shared memories, and I told her that she had to meet Tom, who loves China, having been stationed there before we met.

We went for dinner and started to see a lot of each other. My respect for Jia grew with every meeting. She is what I call one brave woman.

This was her second visit to the United States. Her teaching assignment would run for one year. This was not her first overseas assignment, as she had lectured in Dublin some years back.

Both times, she had to leave her family behind for an entire year to learn about new countries and different cultures. Jia is married and has two adult children. Her daughter has just graduated with a degree in biomedicine and is coming to the United States for graduate studies.

Jia, who is 56, describes her family as part of the Beijing middle class. She and her husband are both university professors. She talks about a fast-changing society, from the formerly communist China to a liberal, Western, industrial nation. She speaks about the difficulties for students in obtaining visas to the United States, and she looks forward to going back to China once her assignment is over.

In the meantime, she is curious and adventurous and, over the last few months, we have discovered many new places together. She is a positive woman with a warm and open personality, who feels at ease wherever she is. Certainly, she has experienced many things over the years, and she has faced countless changes. During the change of her country's political system, she saw a nation opening up to the world.

Jia is very clever and, step by step, she discovers more about America and the Western world. She is not prejudiced or judgmental. Appearances seem superficial to her; she watches with her heart. She is refreshing, like a breeze after a long hot summer.

➢ Liberty

One of the discoveries I made with Jia was the Heritage Center. About 700 people formed the Heritage Community, which is located only a few miles away from Waco. Their tradition and beliefs are linked to those of the first Christians, and they share everything together. We had a good tour and got a lot of insight into their daily living and sharing. The impressive community center, built with their own hands, contains a library that is well stocked with literature and works on science and, in addition, a smaller private library dedicated to history and psychology.

After our tour, we were invited for a home-cooked lunch. Everything seemed harmonious and far removed from the noise and demands of the modern world. The only trace reminding us of modern reality was the occasional ringing of our host's cell phone.

Jia started an interesting conversation about the home schooling of the second and third generations of the Heritage Center. Girls and boys born into this community, founded 30 years ago, are privately educated within the family circle. The primary educator is the mother. She teaches the children math, history, and languages.

I notice that girls in the community, and the young mothers especially, observe us with curiosity. Many were born in the community and had never lived outside of it. I cannot fail to notice that their hairstyles and dresses are a mirror of the early nineteenth century, with their plaits fixed around their heads, their long shirts and skirts, and their flat shoes. Their faces are very plain. The plain looks of the women remind you of the past while the external appearances of the men in the community are no different from those of an everyday modern man.

I am told that the girls learn to cook and clean early. Their daily duties include taking care of the house and the herb garden. They feed the chickens and help in the community. All of them play at least one musical instrument, and the majority sing in the choir.

The girls are very quiet and withdrawn. They have good manners. I was impressed when the girls addressed their fathers as sir, but I started to worry when wives referred to their husbands as sir also.

I asked what happens if a girl wants to marry someone

outside the community, or if it is even possible for a girl to meet anyone from the outside. Well, the reply was that they are free to choose between living in the community and accepting its values, or leaving.

If they decide to live in the community, they obviously have to choose to marry a member from within who shares lasting values that make a marriage work and that go beyond love. Isn't that interesting?

Suppose a woman wants to leave the congregation. Where does she go? It would be difficult for the last two generations of women who have grown up within the safe boundaries of the community. Thirty years ago, their mothers made the free choice to leave society and retreat to the Heritage Community, but the young women of today have been brought up and educated in the community and have had little or no contact with the outside world. They have no higher education. I do not doubt that home education is valid and that many of these girls are bright young women who could attend a university. However, would they be ready to assume their role in society on the outside, to learn to deal with the challenges of life, to earn a living, and to choose a partner?

While their mothers, or at least grandmothers, did have the liberty to choose and decided to give up their identity as women of the twentieth century, their daughters do not have a choice. They have never experienced the outside world. They never chose to be members of the community.

By the time they are 18 and they have spent their entire lives as part of the community, it must be difficult to break out. Leave for what? For a world they are not familiar with, for a reality they do not know because of the lack of media and TV?

The Heritage Community as a sharing and rewarding

environment relies more on women than on men. It is women who assume the very traditional roles of caretakers, educators, and obsequious wives without career ambitions. This is admirable as long as these roles, which involve serious sacrifices, are freely chosen.

What happened to that liberty? What happened to the freedom of choice for today's young girls and women of the Heritage Center?

May 20, 2000

➤ The Magic of a Kind Heart

Today we received a thank-you note. When I opened the tiny envelope, I discovered a beautiful handwritten message: "Thank you for the flowers. They were beautiful. We have enjoyed them for several days. We enjoyed having you all over. Thanks again."

The words—an appreciation for simple flowers we brought to a party two weeks ago—touched my heart,. The host had arranged a farewell party for a company employee who was transferring.

That evening, still at the door, I passed on the wrapped flowers to the host, who obviously was not aware that they were meant for his wife. The flowers were left in the hall and rediscovered the next day. Yesterday, during a Christmas party, the hostess approached us to ask if we had brought the flowers. I replied smilingly that it was just a small gesture.

Now, holding the note, I recall myself fussing in the market about Waco (all the flower shops had been closed on a Saturday afternoon) and whether the flowers (not very many to select from) would be nice enough. How wrong I was proven. It is indeed the very thought and the sincere intention that counts.

I have treasured the thank-you note in my diary ever since. It reminds me that a simple gesture, a small token, can give joy and happiness in a world in which the deep need for sincerity, gratitude, and loving acceptance seldom finds satisfaction. As Mother Teresa said in her book *Mother Teresa: In My Own Words,* "In the developed countries there is a poverty of intimacy, the poverty of spirit, of loneliness, of lack of love. There is no greater sickness in the world today than that one."

➣ Times and Timing of Life

How often have we wished for something so desperately and believed in our hearts that we wouldn't be able to continue on or to do without it for one more day?

How often did that very situation fail to occur even after we wished so desperately for it? How often did we ask for explanations but seemed not to receive the answers?

Often the so greatly desired results only come true when we have let go of our desires and learned that we can, in fact, do without. When we are ready to accept our blessings and not reject them, when we become fulfilled within ourselves as unique individuals, our dreams will come true.

As we are imagining and believing ourselves ready to receive our dreams, while we are actually on the long path toward self-discovery, we feel angry, hurt, and lost because our wishes are not coming true. We are wishing for immediate gratification; we do not want to wait. Unless we accept that the timing of life and of our Higher Power are different from our ideals, we cannot proceed and learn life's lessons.

Life is a kind teacher and, looking back, most of our desires have come true—and we have received many blessings on our journey. We have gotten everything we needed, but certainly not all of it according to our schedule. But let us ask ourselves, would we have been really ready for certain events to happen according to our schedule? Or wasn't it much healthier for them to occur according to heaven's plan? Realistically, at the end of the day, we can certainly state that the natural timing was the better deal for us. Have we ever asked ourselves if we were really ready for certain events to happen when we asked for them to happen? Or do we find out occasionally that a delay in their occurrence— or even them not occurring at all—was a better deal?

If I could I would give you all the colors of the rainbow,
the most brilliant colors of life,
made up of all the colors of the different races.
One Earth combined with the light of the sun
and the shining brightness of the moon
and the stars under the blues of the skies,
one harmonious and balanced picture.
If I could I would give you all the colors of the rainbow,
but I can give only words.
Well-intentioned words can only give so much
unless they are received by open ears
and with an open mind.
Think about these words and they will help you
to transform your thoughts into action.
These words can then move mountains.
They can make you discover the deepest treasure within.
Higher than any mountain and deeper than any sea,
you will discover
Your soul: The window to freedom and peace.

TREASURE THE MOMENT:

The eternal beauty of a sunset: Neither time nor money can bring it back. *Treasure the moment, as its beauty will not return.*

THE COLORS OF THE RAINBOW

... Eternally driven and with a longing forever new,
some of us have visited faraway places.
We have discovered beautiful treasures,
but we do not take the time to enjoy them,
nor are we ready to share.
Never has a single one of our breathless discoveries
kept our attention longer than one moment in time
and never has our search for more been completed.
Restless, we are hunting in unknown directions,
never considering where our journeys might lead
and what our motives are.
However, when we finally take courage to choose
and to discover the most brilliant colors of life
and the highest of all treasures,
we are on the most exciting journey of all time.
We will never look back,
and we will never be hunting again.
The promise is harmony and balance at the
end of the rainbow ...

Visit Daniela Schreier on the World Wide Web:

http://www.thecolorsoftherainbow.com

Bibliography

Beattie, Melodie. *The Language of Letting Go.* Center City, Minn.: Hazelden Foundation, 1990.

Carlson, Richard. *Don't Sweat the Small Stuff.* New York: Hyperion, 1997.

Chu, Chin-Ning. *Do Less, Achieve More: Discover the Hidden Power of Giving In.* New York: HarperCollins Publishers, 1998.

The Dalai Lama, His Holiness. *The Joy of Living and Dying In Peace.* New York: HarperCollins Publishers, 1997.

Frankl, Viktor E. *Man's Search for Meaning.* New York: Pocket Books, 1985.

González-Balado, José Luis. *Mother Teresa: In My Own Words.* New York: Random House, 1997.

Hurley, Joanna. *Mother Teresa: A Pictorial Biography.* New York: Courage Books, 1997.

Miraflower, Norma. *One Woman's Opinion: The Collection.* Singapore: Media Masters Ltd.

Osho. *Life Is a Gift.* New Delhi: Full Circle, 1997.

Ribeiro, Liar. *Viajar en el Tiempo: Recordar el Pasado,*

Crear el Futuro. Barcelona: Ediciones Urbano, 1996.

Sills, Judith. *A Fine Romance: The Passage of Courtship from Meeting to Marriage.* New York: Ballantine Books, 1987.

Van Steenhouse, Andrea. *A Woman's Guide to a Simpler Life.* New York: Three Rivers Press, 1997.

Wholey, Dennis. *The Miracle of Change: The Path to Self-Discovery and Spiritual Growth.* New York: Pocket Books, 1997.

Zuck, Colleen. *Daily Word: Love, Inspiration and Guidance for Everyone.* Kuala Lumpur: Synergy Book International, 1997.

ACKNOWLEDGEMENTS

With her professional insights, Gloria Sweibel helped me to discover a beautiful world, to have confidence in myself, and to focus on life's priorities: harmony, inner freedom, and love.

Special thanks to Mrs. Alfa Ferri Morganti, my *seconda nonna* and Italian grandma. She has a very special place in my heart for being a strong, loving woman who shares my most intimate thoughts.

Gratefulness, joy, and love I am expressing to my Higher Power, the eternal creator of mankind: Thank you for the greatest gift of all: *The inspiration of life and the beauty of living.*

ABOUT THE AUTHOR

Daniela E. Schreier was born in West Germany. She has lived, studied, and worked as an international marketing consultant and public relations specialist all over the world, including Italy, England, Singapore, Malaysia, and India. With a degree in business and psychology, she specializes in stress management.

She resides both in the United States and in Singapore and dedicates her time to writing, inspirational speaking, and leading *The Colors Fund In-dia*. She has recently completed her second book *The Message: An ABC for Women and Men Who Want to Know Us Better,* and is presently at work on a new manuscript for the *The Colors of the Rainbow* series. *The Colors of the Rainbow: About Life and the Beauty of Living* is her debut publication.

Visit her on the World Wide Web at
http://www.thecolorsoftherainbow.com